# HERE'S JOHNNY!

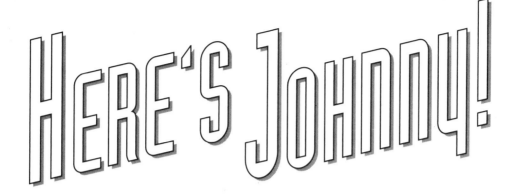

THIRTY YEARS

OF AMERICA'S

FAVORITE

LATE-NIGHT

ENTERTAINMENT

*BY*

STEPHEN COX

HARMONY BOOKS
*New York*

*For my father,*

*who flicked an ash with more flair*

*than Bogey or Gleason*

Published by Harmony Books, a division of Crown Publishers, Inc., 201 East 50th Street, New York, New York 10022. Member of the Crown Publishing Group.

Harmony and colophon are trademarks of Crown Publishers, Inc.

Manufactured in the United States of America

LIBRARY OF CONGRESS CATALOGING-IN-PUBLICATION DATA
Cox, Stephen, 1966–
    Here's Johnny: thirty years of America's favorite late-night entertainment/by Stephen Cox—1st ed.
        p.        cm.
        Includes bibliographical references and index.
        1. Carson, Johnny, 1925–    . 2. Tonight show (Television program)
3. Television personalities—United States—Biography.  I. Title.
PN1992.4.C28C68  1992
791.45'028'092—dc20
[B]                                                                        91-45105
                                                                             CIP

ISBN 0-517-58930-3

10   9   8   7   6   5   4   3   2   1

First Edition

# Contents

# Twenty-one-Star Salute

Envision the ultimate lineup on a perfect *Tonight Show*, or a star-laden Friars Club roast. It might start with a round of toasts from friends and cronies of Johnny Carson. So raise a glass and tip it in honor of America's favorite late-night host, who has been welcome in every American home for thirty years. And now . . . "Cheers, Johnny!"

*❝I don't remember exactly how I met him, but I vividly recall spending an hour with Johnny Carson when we were both in our early twenties in the bar of the old Astor Hotel in Times Square. We were yakking about show business and our hopes and dreams, and I was tremendously impressed with this guy.*

*❝At the end of our talk, I was convinced of two things: I wasn't sure if I was going to make it, but I was dead certain the young man across from me was going to impress the hell out of everybody.*

*❝I think I was right.❞*

—Jack Lemmon

*❝I warned Johnny that nobody could replace Jack Paar. I talked to him like a Dutch uncle. I said, "Don't do it, John! Wait until the first person tries to and then when that bombs—because it surely would—then step in." And I was right, because he's about to lose the show. I don't think he lasted twenty-seven, twenty-eight years.❞*

—Tom Poston

*❝It's a simple fact, that throughout show business history, there has never been such a success story. Who in the world has had thirty years in one spot? It never happened before. There's nothing to compare it to. Sometimes old-timers hang on and they're not so good but the audience likes them and forgives. You don't have to forgive him. He's as good as the day he started.❞*

—Tony Randall

*❝It's a little hard to divorce the Johnny that I love as a friend and watch him objectively. I think he has become a way of life for us, and I don't know what we're gonna do when he leaves, but we can't expect him to devote his entire life to the show.❞*

—Betty White

*❝In the year 3000, Johnny Carson will be the cultural lodestone researchers will covet when studying our popular values.❞* —Dan Aykroyd

The most popular late-night entertainer in the history of television: Johnny Carson in a 1971 publicity portrait. *(courtesy of NBC)*

*Johnny developed into one of the finest comedians on his feet. I've been on his show maybe forty times, probably more. Watching him is great. He's such an asset to the entertainment business. It's a shame he's quitting. It's like a head fallin' off Mount Rushmore.*
—Bob Hope

*He's one of the great, perhaps the greatest, hosts. He can relate to anybody and does it in just the proper way. Some people have just a few levels. He has so many. You watch him with a real old lady, a totally unsophisticated farmer, or even a cute little girl. This is genius. God knows he's the pro of pros.*
—Phyllis Diller

*Over all other hosts, I prefer Johnny Carson. I've always had a lot of fun with Johnny. I attribute many things to Johnny. He's been on for thirty years, and nobody's been able to bump him. His only threat was Rick Dees—only Rick Dees was in a car. He tried to kill Johnny.*
—Jonathan Winters

*I loved being on* The Tonight Show *with Johnny Carson. Nobody listened as good as Johnny. He's also a great actor. He laughed at my jokes like he'd never heard them before.*
—George Burns

*I sure am sorry to see him leave the show. And I join with a great number of people that are sorry. I think he's done an amazing job, and there's a tremendous number of people who have enjoyed him for quite some time.*
—Jimmy Stewart

*He is, he was, and will always be the best there ever was. It's been thirty years of the best television we will ever have. There is not another Johnny Carson . . . unless there'll be another Charlie Chaplin.*
—Jerry Lewis

*I knew Mr. Carson since he was a young man. I knew from the start he could never hold a job. They say he is retiring, but how can you tell?*
*In the 30 years, consider the amount of people who have watched him, he kept a lot of people off the street after 11 at night, but on second thought, those who watched his show from the bed created a lot of criminals, that are running around.*
—Red Skelton

*I've known Johnny Carson for many years. I didn't think it conceivable over the years, that it is possible to be Gentile and genuinely funny. Johnny's a gem, and I owe a great deal of my success to my appearances with him. He shall be missed.*
—Alan King

*I have nothing but the greatest admiration for him. I think that when he quits, it's kind of an end of an era.*
—Jack Paar

*I will personally miss Johnny and thank him in the same breath, for assisting me in my career and for giving me the ultimate exposure in night-time TV. Love you much, Johnny! And I wish you success in whatever you endeavor. Love,*
—Dionne Warwick

*I clearly recall tuning in to see the very first* Tonight Show *with Johnny Carson. It was a rerun. Sincerely,*
—Andy Rooney

*Somebody once said that volume is an important thing when judging talent. If Beethoven had only written* Eroica, *he would be considered one of the great composers, but he wouldn't be considered a genius. It's the amount of things that Beethoven and Mozart turned out; the longevity of creative people like Johnny Carson is a mark of talent. We're gonna miss a friend. And nobody takes the place of a friend.*
—Carl Reiner

*As a veteran of twelve appearances with him and a survivor of about three, all I can say is, I am deeply sorry, and much safer. Cordially,*
—William F. Buckley, Jr.

*I asked Johnny, "Did you have those suits made to order?"*
*He said, "Yes."*
*"Where were you at the time?"*
*Really, Johnny's a charmer. He's helped many of us with our careers. And I thank him.*
—Henny Youngman

*Let me tell you about Johnny Carson. In my lifetime, I've been interviewed by many guys. Some try to draw the humor out, and some I won't even discuss. John is probably the best, or equal to the best. As for fame and fantasy, he's far and above everybody. But I still look at him as a big star and with awe.*
—Buddy Hackett

*There's never been a show or a person who has affected stand-up comedy or as many stand-up comics' lives as Johnny Carson. I predict he'll be back. Maybe on another network a year after he leaves* The Tonight Show, *but he'll be back.*
—Louie Anderson

**NBC Studios**
3000 W. Alameda Ave., Burbank, California

Studio 1

Thursday
October

**1**

1987

Show time
6:30 pm

Guests must
arrive before
5:30 pm

The
TONIGHT SHOW
Starring
JOHNNY CARSON

*25ᵗʰ Anniversary*

0788

---

**NBC Studios**
3000 W. Alameda Ave., Burbank, California

Thursday
August

**1**

1991

No

Cameras

Please!

**The Tonight Show**
Starring
**Johnny Carson**

Minimum age 16
I.D. will be required
Ticket distribution is in excess of
Guests will be seated

Studio 1

Thursday
August

**1**

1991

Show time
5:30 pm

Guests must
arrive before
4:30 pm

---

**NBC Studios**
3000 W. Alameda Ave., Burbank, California

**The Tonight Show**

Starring

**Johnny Carson**

Persons under 18 will not be admitted
Ticket distribution is in excess of studio capac

Studio 1

Wednesday
July

**13**

1977

Show time

---

THE TONIGHT SHOW

ROGER
MOORE

# Introduction

Johnny Carson finally had the Great One, Jackie Gleason, on his show for the first time in 1985. Gleason joked, "I guess I was waiting for this show to become a hit." The host admitted being "an unabashed fan." And I don't mind admitting that I'm an unabashed fan of Johnny Carson. Alas, having never interviewed Jackie Gleason remains a crushing disappointment to me. Lucy is another. But I snagged a chat with Carson and I'm content. President Bush might've been easier to reach by telephone, I realized.

The Carson ensemble took over *The Tonight Show* four years before I was born, and, miraculously, he's become something of a fixture in all of our lives since. For many years, I took for granted that he would remain on television forever. Like midnight itself, he's tuned in automatically. On any given weeknight, he's most likely there inside the blue glow of my set—or sure to return to his post soon. I've watched him in my bedroom, in dorm rooms, basements, bars, hotel rooms, and at friends' homes.

As a fan of the show, any viewer's next step to genuinely experiencing *The Tonight Show* in all its glory is to attend a taping as one of the audience. You have a weird little ditty in the back of your mind all prepared in case Carson steps into the audience for "Stump the Band." Or you hope the "Edge of Wetness" cameras zoom in on *your* face. That's the best outcome, because to appear means you've attained the greatness Andy Warhol once predicted—your own personal fifteen minutes, or in this case, seconds.

Years ago, when I was eighteen and on a trip out West, my pal took me to a taping at NBC—which is nothing short of a must if you're visiting Tinseltown and you're interested in entertainment. Or even if you just like the show. Buddy Hackett was a guest, and that's all I remember about the roster, but what a perfect night. My place in line landed me in the nosebleed section of the studio audience, so steep we hovered above the front row, it seemed. There's nothing like it in life, to see this colorful set, smaller than you envisioned, witness Ed McMahon's booming voice announcing "Heeeeere's Johnny!" while immediately affixing your eyes at the center of the many-colored curtain. After a moment's pause, the Big Man steps out with a wide grin. It really makes you think. *The Tonight Show Starring Johnny Carson* is the last of the Great Television Events and maybe one of the last outposts of television where spontaneous comedy is possible. And to those lucky enough to visit a show, roughly 3 million people over the years, it is indelibly stamped as a great moment, even if it happens five nights a week. There's no more Sullivan, no more *I Love Lucy* filmings, no *Colgate Comedy Hour* or *Cavalcade of Stars*, no Gleason; Jack Benny is gone, and now Carson is stepping down.

**Tickets for *The Tonight Show* were always free to the public.**

I'm a fan, yes, and I wanted to pry still more from the experience; I usually take everything a step further. The next time I attended a taping, I was allowed backstage, where I wandered. My theory has always been: If you look like you know what you're doing, nobody asks questions. I met Doc, Tommy Newsom, took some pictures, and wandered a bit more. I eyed Johnny's coffee mug backstage where a propman had just washed the mugs at a little sink and set them on a cloth to drip dry. No, I couldn't do it.

Johnny had returned to his dressing room immediately, but I peeked around corners for him. I spotted him minutes later, coming down a hall and then some stairs toward me. He was in jeans and a Polo, and surrounded by four guards as he joked and made his way to his shiny Corvette parked just outside the door. I've come to regret not calling for his attention, because I'm sure he would've signed an autograph, but I just stood by and watched, as if I were passing royalty.

Finally, my venture led me to Fred de Cordova in the hallway. He was impeccably fitted in a tan sport coat, carrying a mixed drink in a clear plastic "picnic" cup. When I spoke to him, I startled the omnipresent producer, and he dropped his drink on the carpeted floor. He asked *me* if I was okay, which I thought was unusual. I said sure, and we briefly chatted.

My visit backstage was also a mission: to interest de Cordova in booking yesteryear's comedian Joe Besser, once a member of the Three Stooges, as a guest some night. The Stooges were becoming extremely hot, and Besser, a pal of mine who also hailed from St. Louis, was one of two surviving members of the famed slapstick trio. Besides, de Cordova had directed him in the film, *The Desert Hawk.*

No interest.

Even after a few letters, for some reason *The Tonight Show* did not want to host a Stooge. Not long after, the Three Stooges received their long-deserved star on Hollywood Boulevard. It was 1983, and well over two thousand fans greeted Besser as he accepted the honor for the trio. This was the largest crowd for any "Star Ceremony," surpassing John Wayne's installment, Frank Sinatra's, and everyone else's. (Eventually, Michael Jackson's crowd became the topper.) These high priests of low comedy provoked the hottest comedy renaissance of the 1980s.

Still no interest in a Stooge on *The Tonight Show*.

That didn't diminish my friendship with the show each night. It merely left me wondering. Later in 1989, my book about the Munchkins from the film classic *The Wizard of Oz* was published. For this chronicle, I tracked down all of the surviving members of the 124 midgets—there were only twenty-some left after fifty years—and in my estimation, Carson might have some fun interviewing an original Munchkin. After all, Carson had Adriana Caselotti, the voice of Snow White, on the show when Disney Studios rereleased their gem for the umpteenth time. John Clark Gable, only son of the matinee idol, spoke with Johnny about his father, whom he never met, and the patriarch's legacy left in *Gone With the Wind*. I'm certainly not pillorying any guests, but c'mon . . . how 'bout Prissy (aka actress Butterfly McQueen)? Or Olivia de Havilland would have been a most appropriate guest for the film's fiftieth anniversary. The talent coordinator's choices sometimes bewildered me.

Moreover, even on the golden anniversary of the most beloved film of all time, *The Wizard of Oz*, they wouldn't invite a Munchkin. This only tempted credence in the rumors of "preferred guests," "blacklists," and such that I had always heard.

Oh well. Life went on, and so did the show.

The thought of Johnny's absence is a sad one. My childhood dream, actually the American dream, of trading quips with the King on his show is now nonpractical. Admit it. Everyone has shared my fantasy of stepping out from that curtain to shake Johnny's hand, sitting in the hot seat next to him and making the crowd roar—even better, mak-

**John Clark Gable talks about his late father to a very interested Johnny Carson. *(Globe Photos)***

> A bit tongue-tied one evening, Johnny Carson moved into a commercial saying, "Here's how to relieve an upsex stomach . . . I mean an upset stomach . . . with Sex Lax—Ex-Lax!"

ing Johnny convulse in laughter, pound his desk, or turn his head for fear his dentures will pop out as he busts his gut at my ad-libs.

I would've been a good guest, really! No, I haven't starred in a sitcom or released a pop-hit CD, and admittedly my collection of home-grown vegetables shaped like sexual organs is meager. Maybe I could've held up one of my books, and maybe, just maybe, he'd have uttered that immortal line, "Good stuff," and I'd be rich by the next day.

I'm young, and someday I may have the chance to chat with Jay, or confess something to Donahue, sit on a panel for Sally, or provide fashion tips to Oprah. I've already experienced the thrill of a late-night face-to-face with Larry King on CNN. And Geraldo was merciful to me on the air, thank God, and I think I escaped the show relatively unscathed. Time's up for most of us. My vision of a shot on the show, my fantasy fifteen minutes of ultimate fame promised by Warhol, unfortunately will not be via *The Tonight Show Starring Johnny Carson.*

Thinking about it, though, I may have bested them all. I had the chance to interview *him*, and that, to me, is an adventure I'll never forget.

Regardless of the show's choice or frequency of visitors over the years, it's been nice to have Johnny Carson in my living room—or wherever I may have been. He's always been a good guest. Comfortable, not unsettling. Sometimes hilarious, but never a bore. And he's been there for thirty years. Three decades. I'm gonna miss him.

I'm excited to present this "scrapbook" of sorts, because this book serves as an extension of my fascination with the host, with the show, its remarkable home in history, its years on top, its guests who shined, and its mass appeal; hopefully, it will serve as a delightful time capsule on your bookshelf.

I won't lie by saying this book was a painless endeavor. The nearly insuperable difficulty was getting people to talk about Johnny Carson. Approach people randomly on the street and you might readily prompt twenty minutes about why Johnny appeals to them and their families each night. But ask certain performers who have appeared on the show, or better yet, some close friends of Johnny's, and you might as well forget it.

Shelley Winters was suddenly out of town. Don Rickles decided it might not be a good idea. Robert Blake was reticent, his publicist informed me. Joan Embery was extremely hesitant. Jay Leno felt it would be "inappropriate" for him to comment, with which of course, I couldn't disagree more. Roseanne and Tom Arnold barred any personal comments. Dick Carson, Johnny's brother, wouldn't respond to my handwritten plea given to him by his barber during one Tuesday morning appointment in July. Magician Dean Dill, "personal instructor to Mr. Carson" who has appeared on *The Tonight Show,* would not expound on Johnny's sleight-of-hand talents. Instead, the part-time magician/barber sicced on me a pseudo-agent, who quizzed me as if I were a witness in the Senate's Thomas-Hill hearings.

Get this: Performer John Davidson, who guest-hosted the show many times during the 1970s, instantly admitted it was fabulous for his career but refused to be quoted saying it. Steve Allen's secretary wanted sample chapters. "Would you believe . . ." even Don Adams, TV's secret agent Maxwell Smart, wouldn't respond? The list expanded, and finally, when all was said and done, I concluded that those who felt comfortable and confident in their relationship with "Mr. Carson" spoke; those who did not, didn't.

It was a funny realization. So many of those interviewed and those who wouldn't go on record walked on eggshells when it came to Carson. They carefully chose their words and definitely made it clear they did not want to jeopardize a good thing. Carson was their friend and associate, and he had been soured by books about him in the past. There was no mistaking this. Half of my time was spent explaining this project: This book delves more into the career than the life of Johnny Carson, America's favorite ambassador into Dreamland. This book celebrates the three decades, the nearly six thousand shows Johnny Carson gave us. In other words, it will reveal more about his work than about his personal life. And he has even said he doesn't mind criticism of his work. When you start digging personal dirt, though, it alerts this comedian, who's been described as an "elaborately wired security system."

So many articles and multifaceted essays in diverse forums—from *TV Guide* to *Playboy*, from Barbara Walters to *60 Minutes*—have attempted to tap the inner being within this Johnny Carson fellow. They all claim to finally solve the puzzle, "What is the real Johnny Carson like?" In most cases, they fail to reveal anything much. And do you know what? That strategically constructed privacy is half the Carson appeal and mystique that kept the country watching for thirty years. Indeed, he is one of Hollywood's biggest stars—possibly more widely recognized than the presidents of the United States. And yet, it's a paradox: He has remained one of the most private public figures.

Regardless of the barriers, the criticism, the lack of enthusiasm displayed by many who work with Johnny Carson, I was determined to make this book work. In assembling a pictorial history such as this, I wanted to surprise myself—by digging up material that I hadn't seen, facts I hadn't known. And then present it to the public as a gift, in the form of this book—not a eulogy to Carson's career but a celebration.

Naturally, we all have our favorite moments, and maybe this *Tonight Show* companion will spark some for you, but I trust everyone will be able to open these pages and say, "Do you remember when . . . ?"

Maybe you're an unabashed fan?

*Stephen Cox*

# Johnny Carson Is . . .

He's been called many things over the last three decades. Here are a few of the more interesting phrases pinned on the comedian. Johnny Carson is . . .

❝ the man who has logged more hours in our bedrooms than many a lover . . . ❞

❝ agelessly boyish, outrageously wealthy, and greatly popular. ❞

❝ the chief of chitchat. ❞

❝ Master of Monologues. ❞

❝ . . . the most powerful figure in Hollywood. ❞

❝ the man America has loved to go to bed with. ❞

❝ . . . a textbook American hero. ❞

❝ pioneer of the three-day work week. ❞

❝ The highest-paid entertainer in the history of television. ❞

❝ Johnny-on-the-spot with an instant retort. ❞

❝ . . . a walking paradox: open, boyish, engaging and relaxed on-camera; aloof, defensive, parsimonious and paranoid off-camera. ❞

❝ . . . the third engineer to run the crack train that is *The Tonight Show.* ❞

❝ . . . a mighty distraction in the nation's bedroom. ❞

❝ . . . choirboy-gone-wrong. ❞

❝ the nation's security blanket. ❞

❝ . . . a kingpin of our popular culture. ❞

❝ . . . like a Peck's Bad Boy with white hair. ❞

❝ a presence in our minds, at times more real than even the important politicians and leaders of our land. ❞

❝ a jingling bag of money for NBC. ❞

❝ . . . both a quintessentially midwestern boy and an urbane Hollywood sophisticate. ❞

❝ the sixty-year-old man with the Boy Scout face. ❞

❝ part of our cultural furniture . . . ❞

❝ an elaborately wired security system. ❞

"Carson is a master of the cozy pace and mood that he believes are appropriate for the muzzy midnight hours."

*Time* magazine, May 19, 1967

---

❝ America's most private comedian. ❞

❝ one of the fastest 'thinkers' on his feet. ❞

❝ the comic consciousness of the United States. ❞

❝ perhaps the nation's most prominent political commentator. ❞

❝ Nebraska's best-known product. ❞

❝ America's town crier. ❞

# Talking with Johnny

This time the tables were turned.

"Hello, Steve?" the voice questioned, while I was eating dinner. "This is Helen in Johnny Carson's office. Mr. Carson has a few minutes to speak with you now if you'd like."

Like? I couldn't believe she asked that. I wouldn't have been more startled if Mikhail S. Gorbachev had called. Nearly in a state of shock, yet conscious of my moves, I switched phones, sat at my desk, and started to interview my late-night idol. The Silver Fox. King of the Night. Johnny.

It was about 4:00 P.M. in Burbank, and Johnny Carson was in his office preparing for his 5:30 P.M. curtain. I'd told him in a fax that preceded that a few riddles had emerged from my research about his career and the show. Reiterating now, I noted my wish that this book be favorable to him.

"Well, that'll be new," he snapped lightheartedly.

I told him I had no interest in digging up dirt about his personal life; I'd just like to inquire about a few things. "All right. Go ahead," he said.

He was polite, quiet—which I'm told he usually is in interviews—and serious. I was hurried and tongue-tied. I imagined him sitting on a nice couch, scanning papers with the show's monologue spread in front of him, his head cocked, with the telephone squeezed between ear and shoulder.

Where is Barbara Walters when you need her? I could have used one of her parapsychological questions: "If you were a carnival ride, which one would you be?" Instead, my mind raced through a hundred topics I could have approached, but mostly I held to the agenda stated in my letter. After all, I must have done *something* right, because I had been told by his closest associates that he was accepting no interview requests at all. We discussed a variety of topics before I thanked him for his time.

He had narrated *Stuart Little*, an animated film I watched in grade school. Based on the E. B. White book for children, this sort of claymation adventure about a mouse was a favorite with me and my classmates. He recorded that in 1966, the year I was born, I told him. I had said the right thing. His voice sounded as though he was happy with the topic.

"Somebody came to me from PBS, and they were going to use it in schools, which they did," he began. "I just did it for a lark. I knew the story, of course. The producer came to me, I can't think of his name, and we did it in about a day. I think it won some kind of an award from the educational system or something."

I wondered if he was a fan of E. B. White, who also wrote *Charlotte's Web*.

"Yes, very much so. I think his book *Elements of Style* is one of the best books written." I had a copy at my elbow, worn and ragged from my college days. It's sort of a bible for writers.

Johnny with Stuart Little, the animated character adapted from an E. B. White story. The Carson-narrated special, *The World of Stuart Little*, aired in 1966 and has been distributed to schools across America as a popular children's viewing selection ever since. *(from the author's collection)*

Johnny's a fan of another person whom I also greatly admired. It's no secret Jack Benny was his idol, and I asked him to single out something Benny had taught him.

"Oh, that's easy," he said. "Editing and timing. Sure, how to edit sketches, and timing."

Was there another comedian who greatly influenced him?

"It's hard to single out one," he said. "I grew up in the radio days. There are a lot of people I admired. Fred Allen for his wit. I admire Benny. I admired Hope in those days. A lot of those comedians. I'm a Laurel and Hardy fan. I suppose when somebody starts, they unconsciously or consciously steal a little bit from everybody, and then later on you evolve your own style. But when you're starting, everybody grabs a little bit. Jackie Gleason admitted that he took a lot of his stuff from Oliver Hardy, but eventually it became Jackie Gleason."

I mentioned that I had detected a bit of Don Adams in him and him in Don Adams. He thought a moment.

"I think that's true," he said, but not with much certainty. "And that probably goes back to Groucho Marx. You know, the kind of satirical throwaway line." This, among other explanations he provided, revealed a side of Johnny Carson I didn't know. His eye for comedy and consequently his performance is unquestionably apt. But his ability to analyze and interpret the art is something many comedians are just not able to do. He really is a serious student of comedy.

Moving swiftly to other topics, I asked him why he hasn't done some of the more popular routines recently, like the "Tea-Time Movies," Aunt Blabby, or Floyd R. Turbo.

"We haven't done Turbo in quite a while," he said, choosing this character to expound on. "Once you cover so many, you have to find the right subject. It's not enough just to go out and do him to be doing him. He has to illustrate a point of view, and we went through a lot of them. Whether it was the National Rifle Association or socialized medicine or women in the army or whatever."

I secretly speculated that as a comedian now in his mid-sixties he no longer wanted to put on the kooky costumes, raise his voice a few octaves, or throw on a wig for Aunt Blabby. Or Art Fern, or el Moldo. Or any other wild characters that once made that spot on the show so fun. It's difficult now to imagine him lying on a gym mat with Richard Simmons experimenting with new exercises, twisting, jumping, and stretching.

Most likely, Carson knew I would inquire about his imminent departure months away. Above all, I wanted to approach this topic, so I reminded him of the time he quoted Jimmy Durante saying, "Let the audience let you know when to exit." I asked: Are you assuming the audience is telling you it's time?

Lore has it that golf pro Arnold Palmer appeared on the show one night and Johnny Carson asked him if his wife did anything to wish him luck before his tournaments. Palmer explained, "She washes my balls." "I guess that makes your putter stand up," Carson replied.

"Basically what I think he meant was, when the audience doesn't *show up*, it's time to pack it in," he said, that likable Nebraska chuckle in his voice. "The audience will let you know when it's time to quit. That's *not* why I decided to retire from *The Tonight Show*. I didn't want to get to that point. I'd rather leave while the show was still hot. And it's time. There are other things to do."

Any plans? Vegas again, maybe?

"Oh, I may go in concert," he said. "I haven't been in concert for ten years, and that's always an option. There's other specials I might want to do. Maybe comedy in politics or something, when the timing is right."

Anxious not to lose my connection before I had verified what I thought must be his finest line, I played straight man with one last question. I asked him what he wanted for his epitaph. Without hesitating a second, he answered: "I'll Be Right Back."

And on that final night, when he steps through that curtain for the last time, will he tell the audience he'll be right back?

"I don't know," he said, briefly quiet, perhaps thinking. "I haven't figured out what we're going to do for the final show yet, or even if we'll have a studio audience. No, I don't know. We're not going to do it in prime time. It will be the same time slot. We started there, and that's where we should finish."

# Trademarks

You might recall having seen Johnny . . .

1. Grab the knot of his tie and straighten it.

2. Apply his index finger to his upper lip when talking seriously.

3. Tap his pencil on the cigarette box or the rim of his coffee mug.

4. Flip a pencil in the air and catch it—sometimes.

5. Keep his hands in his pockets while his chest is inflated during the monologue.

6. Hold his hands behind his back, throwing his chest out (while standing for the monologue).

7. Scratch the back of his hand as though it itched.

8. Crane his neck.

9. Yell "Whoopee!" after his golf swing and the audience was applauding his monologue.

10. Shoot his index finger into the air like a gun.

11. Scratch the back of his ear.

12. Scratch his temple.

13. Lick his thumb when turning pages during a desk routine.

14. Tweak the bottom of his nose.

15. Hold up his hand, waving the audience, which has been roaring unceasingly, to a halt. ("No, no . . .")

16. After the monologue, give the "come hither" gesture with his hands at his waist, sparking more applause.

17. Twitch one eye when he's noticeably annoyed.

18. Occasionally raise his voice an octave as if in transformation from puberty. "You know . . ." (clearing his throat).

19. Wink (as to say, "I'm just teasing," or "You're doing fine.")

20. Swing a golf club to signal the end of the monologue.

*("We'll be right back, folks.")*

**Perhaps Carson's most infamous trade mark: straightening his tie.**

# 1

# The Evolution of
# The Tonight Show

**❝ *I don't want to sit there when I'm an old man. I don't envision sitting there in my sixties. I think that would be wrong.* ❞**
—Johnny Carson,
*Rolling Stone*, 1979

On Johnny's fifteenth-anniversary show, NBC president Robert Mulholland appeared on the live special and congratulated Johnny: "It's good to be here. This show, as you know, means a lot to NBC. Not only to the people who work here, but to all the people who watch NBC across the country. This is only fifteen, and we'll go for fifteen more if you will."

Carson thought aloud, "Fifteen more, let's see . . . I would be eligible for the Motion Picture Home."

No one knows whether Johnny had that visionary night on his mind when he informed NBC that he would leave Tonight on May 22, 1992, the job he began on October 1, 1962, at age thirty-six. Directly following, a flurry of activity and a bated breath of expectation left the network in confusion.

There was ambivalence whether Johnny would actually leave or not. He had threatened to quit the show several times before in the wake of contractual disputes and other matters over the years. Way back in 1970, he told the Associated Press: "After seventeen years, I'm getting a little tired of it. I don't think I can bring anything new to it and it gets a little tougher all the time to do it, and I want to keep the standard of the show up."

His solutions were many, over the years. With Johnny as the show's artist, he shaped the show, shortened it, moved it, but all the while he steadily kept it thriving as a consistent entity of quality network programming with more than pleasing ratings. In exchange, he collected a more than pleasing paycheck. He told *TV Guide* in 1981, "When I was thinking of quitting once, I got a wonderful letter from Kenneth Tynan, who was a big fan of mine. It was very flattering, and he said, 'You know, Picasso didn't do much besides paint, and Astaire was pretty content to dance most of his life. . . .'" Carson conceded to the obvious. He loved what he did, so he stuck with it.

This time, however, Johnny was not kidding. This was not a ruse to hike his salary, or a ploy for added ratings. He's not quitting this time; he's retiring from the show.

Three decades have raced by, it seems, with Carson as a mainstay to the late-night audiences. Only now, it doesn't seem so late. It's more acceptable to be up at the hour of Johnny. After May 22, 1992, for a while anyway, it will be the hour of Jay Leno, cho-

The twenty-sixth anniversary show, in October 1988, gathered the ghosts of guest-host past, when David Letterman, Garry Shandling, and Jay Leno appeared to join the celebration and congratulate Johnny. *(Wide World Photo)*

sen by NBC to take Carson's scepter and run into the night as *The Tonight Show*'s newest host. The era of Johnny Carson, his *Tonight Show* chapter, will close, on a tearful spring night when possibly the largest audience in television history will bid the host farewell with rocketing ratings.

*TV Guide* reported in June 1991, shortly after Leno's appointment, that "NBC executives Warren Littlefield and John Agoglia flew from Los Angeles to New York so that they could personally tell the iconoclastic host of *Late Night with David Letterman* that they had chosen Leno as Carson's replacement. Letterman was reported shocked at the news. His shock turned to anger, then hurt."

At NBC, the powers making the decisions felt that Leno, permanent guest host since the autumn of 1987, was the logical choice. His tenure already established him with younger audiences, which could result in a smooth transition.

One behind-the-scenes figure at NBC says Letterman was "angrier than anyone had ever seen him." Another report run from an Associated Press story quoted a source describing Letterman as "fit to be tied."

Within a few weeks, Letterman reportedly mellowed and made a few jokes on his own show.

"You know what this means to us?" Letterman quizzed his sidekick Paul Shaffer. "We get 'Stump the Band.' And I'm negotiating for Aunt Blabby. Keep your fingers crossed. We don't know if they'll just be handed over or what. . . ." A few months later, after conversations with Carson, Letterman appeared as Johnny's guest, where Carson made light of the news stories.

**Despite news reports to the contrary, David Letterman claimed he was not mad that Jay Leno had been appointed Johnny's successor, and said to Johnny, "Realistically, if it were not for you, I wouldn't have a show."**
**(Globe Photos)**

## Tonight Show Timeline

May 29, 1950, to August 24, 1951: *Broadway Open House* (alternating hosts: Jerry Lester and Morey Amsterdam)

August 27, 1951, to September 24, 1954: *The Steve Allen Show*

September 27, 1954, to January 25, 1957: *Tonight!* (starring Steve Allen)

January 28, 1957, to July 26, 1957: *Tonight! America After Dark* (various hosts)

July 29, 1957, to March 30, 1962: *The Tonight Show* (starring Jack Paar)

April 2, 1962, to September 28, 1962: *The Tonight Show* (interim with various hosts)

October 1, 1962, to April 1972: *The Tonight Show Starring Johnny Carson* (emanating from New York City)

May 1, 1972, to May 22, 1992: *The Tonight Show Starring Johnny Carson* (emanating from Burbank, California)

CARSON: *There were rumors you were gonna firebomb NBC....*
LETTERMAN: *Well, I hate waitin' in lines, but I'd do it.*

Letterman continued: "No, I'm not angry. Not angry at NBC. Not angry at Jay Leno . . . Now if the network had come to me and said, 'Dave, we'd like you to have this show and then a week later they said, 'Dave we don't want you to have this show,' you could be angry. I was never, never angry.

"Now, would I like to have this show? Oh yeah! And from what I know of you, a guy can make a pretty comfortable living doing this show."

Nightclub comic Jerry Lester said the same thing, when NBC programming genius Sylvester "Pat" Weaver contacted him in 1950 about pioneering a television show. This program would be on late, quite unusual for the limited television audiences during the period, but Weaver was one of the few who trusted the concept that viewers would indeed stay up and tune in if there was something to watch. He didn't want anything too serious—a flavor Carson strived to maintain—and Lester, he felt, was the perfect host.

*Broadway Open House*, TV's grandaddy of all informal talk-and-variety television shows, premiered on May 29, 1950, and lasted until August 24, 1951. Sponsored by the Anchor Hocking glass company, which produced beer bottles, the show ran for a brief tenure on live television, but the implantation was historical. It was a landmark in television when it was first flashed before the public. It was the forerunner for Steve Allen, for Jack Paar, and for Johnny Carson. It was television's answer to the test-pattern blues.

After its premiere, *TV Forecast* magazine's reader poll named it first place in comedy and variety:

**Regulars on TV's *Broadway Open House*, the forerunner of *The Tonight Show*. L–R: announcer Wayne Howell, emcee Jerry Lester, bandleader Milton DeLugg, and comedienne Dagmar. *(courtesy of Milton DeLugg)***

*The bouncy, roly-poly Jerry Lester, who took the show over for three of the five nights each week, was considered the real spirit and brains of the show as well as its chief performer. It was he who decided what was right and not right, who was to go on and for how long. It was he who hired a big blonde model, Jenny Lewis, and gave her the famous name of Dagmar.*

*The Chicago-born Lester, a puckish veteran of stardom in vaudeville, radio, night clubs and Broadway revues, knew he had a good thing with* Broadway Open House.

Comedy writer Morey Amsterdam was the alternate host of *Broadway Open House,* on Monday and Wednesday nights while Lester emceed the other three. There was not much of a format, says Amsterdam, who weighed in at 180 pounds in those days, compared to his 120 pounds today. "It was like a little stock company," he says. "We had our own people on the show. We wrote our own sketches but ad-libbed most of the show."

Regulars on the program included Dave Street, Jane Harvey, the Mello Larks, Bob Warren, Elaine Dunn, Jack Leonard, Buddy Greco, Ray Malone, the Honeydreamers, Dell and Abbott, Maureen Cannon, Frank Gallop, and Barbara Nichols.

Amsterdam describes one of the program's biggest burdens in those days:

"There was no such thing as videotape. We went on live, and kinescopes were made and distributed," he prefaces. "And we had to have a studio audience. Where in New York, at midnight, are you gonna find a studio audience? Radio was big now, so I went out in the halls and a whole line would be waiting to get into *The Fred Allen Show.* By eight o'clock, everyone was on their way home.

"So I went to a bus company and I told them, 'You know, television is new and everybody wants to see what a studio looks like,'" he says with his solution in mind. "I said, 'Tell your people when you take 'em to the nightclubs and the hot spots in New York, the big thing is to see a television show!' We filled it up with people visiting on buses."

Musical director on the show Milton DeLugg says that when the show started, it instantly became a "remarkable hit. It was the only thing on at eleven at night." The program lasted an hour, with commercials. When it became hot, the whole show visited other cities to originate the broadcast, such as Detroit, but mostly its home was Studio 6B at NBC in New York—the same studio Johnny Carson eventually called home before he relocated *The Tonight Show* out to Burbank, California, permanently

DeLugg's band consisted of himself on the accordion, and someone on piano, guitar, bass, drums, and a trumpet. "The accordion was received wonderfully then," he says. "After a few years, it was not considered too noble an instrument. It's a shame. Everybody did put-downs on it." Eventually, DeLugg's band had a few hits popularized

Jerry Lester, the nightclub comic who became TV's first late-night TV host. *(Personality Photos, Inc.)*

Comedy writer Morey Amsterdam, who went on to fame as Buddy Sorrell on TV's *Dick Van Dyke Show*, was the alternating host on *Broadway Open House* in 1950. *(courtesy of Morey Amsterdam)*

on the show and finally got placed on the Hit Parade: "Hoop Dee Do," "Orange Colored Sky" (which was recently recorded by Natalie Cole), and "Be My Life's Companion."

The real sensation of *Broadway Open House* was Jenny Lewis (real name Virginia Ruth Engor) who became known simply as "Dagmar." Writer Wambly Bald wrote in 1957 of the "phenomenal rise of Jenny Lewis . . . [a] junoesque blonde with outstanding natural endowments . . . first given $25 per performance just to sit on the high stool and decorate the set. Then she was given a few "dumb blonde" lines to say, and the public went wild. The name Dagmar became synonymous with sex appeal at its grandest. . . . Her fan mail was enormous. In a matter of months, she was getting $1,250 a week."

Reportedly, Jerry Lester, the man who discovered her, began to envy her popularity on the show, which led to a feud between the two and ultimately the demise of the whole program. He denied it, but Amsterdam and DeLugg both called Lester an "egomaniac," citing his demands as the primary reason the program was halted.

"Jerry was a talented comedian," Amsterdam notes. "He said to me one day, 'Starting next year, I'm gonna do the show just once a week. Then I'll do it once a month. And once a year. And they'll be waiting for me.' He was out of his mind."

The show's producer, Hal Friedman, indicated in a 1957 interview that egos began to clash and the spontaneity had vanished within a year. "In the beginning," Friedman said, "the show shaped up as a well-balanced unit . . . just a running order and a premise every performance. As soon as individual performers stood out from the others, the balance was destroyed."

Jerry Lester continued to act in television and in nightclubs and retired to Florida with his wife in the 1970s. He was reunited with regulars on the show, Milton DeLugg included, for a taping of the *Tomorrow* show in the 1970s, but has remained retired since.

Milton DeLugg went on to direct musical segments for many NBC "house specials,"

he calls them, Macy's Parades, Orange Bowl Parades, and Junior Miss Pageants. He returned to his roots as music director—this time for *The Tonight Show* in New York, when Skitch Henderson left the show in 1966. He stayed briefly until Doc Severinsen was named music director in 1967. The TV themes he's composed include "Rollercoaster" (theme to TV's *What's My Line?*), and the music for *The Dating Game*, *The Newlywed Game*, and *The Gong Show*. He lives in Los Angeles.

Morey Amsterdam continued his writing career, which began in vaudeville and radio, and successfully made the transition into television. He is, perhaps, best known to television audiences as the lovable jokester Buddy Sorrell on TV's *The Dick Van Dyke Show*.

Legends of late-night TV met for the first time at a taping of NBC's Sixtieth Anniversary special in 1986. L–R: Jerry Lester, Jack Paar, Johnny Carson, and Steve Allen. *(courtesy of NBC)*

# Enter: Steve Allen

*The Steve Allen Show* actually began as a local presentation in June 1953 on WNBT-TV, the NBC flagship station in New York. Sponsored by Ruppert Breweries, the show later became a network offering retitled *Tonight!* Beginning September 27, 1954, it was expanded to 105 minutes on the air, nightly.

During this tenure, the basic format of *The Tonight Show* as we know it was established by the highly prolific comedian and writer Steve Allen. The show had an opening monologue, a segment where Allen would go into the studio audience (like the "Stump the Band" bits), and a simple set of a desk and chair was initiated. Allen established the "one guest" show, spotlighting a solo personality for the show, the first being Carl Sandburg. Moreover, and much to the chagrin of visiting actors to the program, Allen established the flat fee he paid his guests. Commonly known as "scale," it was the uniform price he set for everyone, which raised a stink. Ed Sullivan paid top dollar for guests, while Allen remained on an even scale for everyone.

There were guest stars, in addition to semiregulars such as Gene Rayburn (who went on to host the many seasons of *Match Game* the TV game show), Steve Lawrence, Eydie Gormé, Andy Williams, Skitch Henderson and His Orchestra, Bill Wendell the announcer (who has made more of a name as David Letterman's announcer), and Hy Averback.

In addition to special features, comedy skits, and audience participation, a regular news update was provided halfway through the program. The show was produced live. At the same time, Allen starred in a prime-time series, and by 1956, caught in the web of hectic schedules and conflicting engagements, Allen cut back his *Tonight!* appearances to Wednesday through Friday. A series of guest hosts filled in the remaining days until the brilliant TV pioneer Ernie Kovacs accepted the position as permanent guest-host for Allen's days off.

"For most of his laughs," wrote TV historian Bart Andrews, "Steve Allen relied on his guests. They were his springboard to humor. Once one of them showed up with a few live ducks in a wading pool, so Steve went wading too.

"When two old ladies in his '*Tonight!*' audience kept talking noisily to each other during the performance, Steve turned the problem into a plus. He recalls: 'I think the heart of all humor is something going wrong. So I slanted all my talk that night to these two old ladies. I could have had a page throw them out, but instead I made them a part of the show.'"

Allen introduced to audiences some new comedians, including Lenny Bruce and Shelly Berman. Above all, with his wide-ranging improvisational skills that are greatly imitated by David Letterman these days, Allen pulled in a sizable audience during his tenure as host.

Actor Tony Randall recalls Steve Allen's show with fondness as he describes one of his guest-hosting chores:

"In those days it was live, and the show was two hours and fifteen minutes long," Randall explains. "I was playing in *Inherit the Wind* at the Broadway Theater on Forty-first Street, and *Tonight!* was from the Hudson Theater on Forty-fourth Street. My cur-

Steve Allen: the first host of *Tonight! (courtesy of Steve Allen)*

tain came down at eleven-fifteen, and the *Tonight!* show began at eleven-fifteen P.M. There was no way to get a limo or cab through those streets at that hour when all the theaters were letting out. There was only one way to do it, and that was to run, literally run, through the streets.

"The announcer, Bill Wendell, would cover for me until I got there," Randall says, laughing. "A couple of times they had the cameras out there on the streets so the audience could see me running. I'd be running as fast and as hard as a man could run."

On January 25, 1957, Allen hosted his final *Tonight!* show because the network ordered him to concentrate on his Sunday variety series, which battled the steady ratings of Ed Sullivan. Allen was, by comparison, a good match for Sullivan.

# The Interim

## Tonight! America After Dark

After Steve Allen departed his late-night spot in January 1957, the time slot was replaced by an experiment, which utterly flopped in the evening hours. It was ill conceived and diffuse, and more of a magazine show than what its predecessors had established as welcomed entertainment in the wee hours.

The show featured a group of correspondents who broadcasted from different cities. The original lineup included Hy Gardner, Bob Considine, and Earl Wilson in New York; Irv Kupcinet in Chicago; and Paul Coates and Vernon Scott in Los Angeles. Music was provided by the Lou Stein Trio.

The show resembled *Today* in format, with a mixture of entertainment and hard news coverage. The show was dumped by NBC on July 26, 1957, when the ratings plunged.

# The Jack Paar Years

Things took a drastic turn when young CBS game-show and talk-show host Jack Paar took hold of the new version of NBC's late-night show, rudely interrupted by *Tonight! America After Dark* in the months prior. Paar was introduced on the show on July 29, 1957, and American television would never see another host grab the country with such power until Johnny Carson gained speed during the late 1960s.

The title changed a few times. Originally called *Tonight* (without the exclamation point of the Steve Allen era), it was later officially retitled *The Jack Paar Tonight Show*. This new host's first task was to win back ratings and sponsorship that Steve Allen had worked so hard to build. His job of selling himself in this time slot was also ahead. He was not a stand-up comic, or an actor.

About Jack . . . many, many things can be extrapolated regarding this unique, intricate television personality who constantly had his dukes up. First, he admits he's a conversationalist. "I don't think of myself as an interviewer," he said recently in a rare interview. "That's something I did just to fill time. I was just as happy if I were alone."

He was highly emotional on his program. His audiences never knew what to expect when tuning in, or witnessing a taping. He was a master of the insult, but he smiled when he jabbed. As writer Cheryl Lavin put it, when audiences watched Paar, they might wonder, "Whom would Paar attack? Who would walk off the show? Would he do another episode of beat the press—or would it be Mr. Weepers tonight? There was a built-in excitement based on his unpredictability."

The show, said Newsweek, was "Russian roulette with commercials."

His theme music, "Everything's Coming Up Roses," would fill the studio, and announcer Hugh Downs would say, "Here's Jack." His delivery was not past stammering through a monologue or painstakingly telling his favorite story. He might describe his latest trip to the dentist. His chats were real, rambling, personal, and most importantly—like the medium of television itself—intimate. "Daughter Randy got her first bra today," he'd say. And then he'd cry. He cried a lot.

"I am emotional," he said recently from his home in Connecticut, where he and his wife, Miriam, retired. "If you were talking for nine hours a week—don't forget I did an hour and forty-five minues live, not like they are doing now: an hour on tape with twelve or thirteen writers. I had two, possibly three, writers at one time.

"And there you are for an hour and forty-five minutes at night. Naturally, if you're creative and humorous, you talk about things you know about.

Jack Paar, the charming and emotionally packed personality who hosted the *Tonight Show* during its Camelot years, 1957–62. *(courtesy of Jack Paar)*

Things that happened to you with your daughter, with your dogs, with your friends. Or my experiences with the Kennedys or the Nixons or the Fords. I think the emotional thing is highly played up. It's not to say there weren't emotional comments. But that's the way I am. Now and then."

He's a good name-dropper, with the credentials to do so. He began with a crew of regulars, but only two remained to the end: announcer and sidekick Hugh Downs and bandleader José Melis, Paar's former army buddy. Others who stopped by the show from time to time included Dody Goodman, Tedi Thurman; semiregulars who might stop by to chat included Elsa Maxwell, Zsa Zsa Gabor, Hans Conreid, Peggy Cass, Charley Weaver, and Mary Margaret McBride.

His guests were great talkers, entertainers, wits, and thinkers. Minds such as Oscar Levant, Richard Nixon, Selma Diamond, Burl Ives, Hermione Gingold, and a young senator named John Kennedy and his brother Bobby even appeared on the show. Fans of Judy Garland could always rely on an amusing storytelling session from the legendary singer. Paar was one of the few to draw that talent from Garland, who naturally favored audiences with songs as well. He and Garland were pals.

Skitch Henderson, the bandleader for both Paar and
Carson from 1962 to 1966.
*(from the author's collec-
tion)*

He liked unusual guests—not professional studio guests with rehearsed conversation. He also hated anyone unjustly hogging his camera. Once, comic Jack E. Leonard
insulted Paar for nearly ten minutes on the air. Then Paar stopped him with this line:
"Jack Leonard got a lot of laughs tonight. And you'll be seeing a lot more of him. But
not on my show."

Paar also introduced a large group of talented folks on his show who went on to do
wonderful things in the entertainment business: Phyllis Diller, Bob Newhart, Carol
Burnett, Barbra Streisand, Bill Cosby, Liza Minnelli, and the Beatles—yes, the Fab
Four. He didn't introduce the group as an appearing act, you see, but he did feature
them in a videotape of unusual acts hailing from England; this was prior to their na-

tional debut with Ed Sullivan, that threw American teens into a frenzy. He's proud of that edge he has on Sullivan, slight as it may be.

There were front-page feuds between Paar and the press (Walter Winchell, Dorothy Kilgallen); between Paar and other entertainers (Mickey Rooney, Steve Allen, Ed Sullivan); between Paar and his employers (regarding censorship, the program's length). No one was safe, it seemed. And yet—everyone in America tuned in. His ratings went through the roof. When he started, his lineup grew from sixty-two stations carrying his show and pushed it to 115 affiliates. The feuds always helped the ratings, because audiences would return as to a soap opera, to see the next installment of Paar.

Exceedingly popular, sensitive, and emotional on television in the 1950s and 60s, Jack Paar displays photographs of a few of his noted guests: (clockwise) Robert Kennedy, Richard Nixon, Judy Garland, Richard Burton, and John F. Kennedy. *(courtesy of Jack Paar)*

Johnny Carson and Jack Paar had their career similarities, but not regarding their style of hosting. *(Personality Photos, Inc.)*

In 1960, Paar walked off his show abruptly because of a censorship dispute with NBC over a "water closet" joke he had told. NBC censors, considering the story in bad taste, edited the tapes before airtime, which enraged the fighting host. He returned after a month and expressed his regret, but the news had made headlines everywhere. Large headlines. Later, he announced he would quit as master of ceremonies because of the rigors of the hour-and-forty-five-minute show. He wanted NBC to cut the time, but it refused. "I'm doing more television than Gleason, Gobel, Allen and Berle combined," he told the press in September 1958. "I don't want more money. I just want less time."

Johnny's guest one night was a woman who ran a cattery, which is like a cat kennel, for the care and sale of cats. He said after the monologue, ". . . and in a little while we're going to bring out a lady who runs a cat house."

On March 29, 1962, the forty-three-year-old massively popular host cried three times as he left his show, and left America wondering how he could be replaced.

# Interim II

## *The Tonight Show* (April 2, 1962–September 28, 1962)

While Johnny Carson, the appointed successor to Jack Paar, was forced to complete his contract with producer Don Fedderson and ABC-TV's *Who Do You Trust?*, a succession of substitute hosts filled in. Announcers were Hugh Downs (who stayed until August, then became host of Today), Jack Haskell, and Ed Herlihy. The orchestra was led by Skitch Henderson. Hosts during this period were Art Linkletter, Joey Bishop, Bob Cummings, Merv Griffin, Jack Carter, Jan Murray, Peter Lind Hayes, Mary Healy, Soupy Sales, Mort Sahl, Steve Lawrence, Jerry Lewis, Jimmy Dean, Arlene Francis (the first female guest host), Jack E. Leonard, Hugh Downs, Groucho Marx, Hal March, and Donald O'Connor.

The format was relatively unchanged, and the six-month hiatus while awaiting the arrival of Johnny Carson was uneventful at most. The network reported the ratings were steady, and they did not drop.

# "Johnny's Theme"

Paul Anka was already an international teen idol with hits like "Diana" and "Put Your Head on My Shoulder" topping the charts when he met Johnny Carson for the first time in England in 1961. Anka was filming a television special, *An Evening with Paul Anka*, for Granada Television in London when producers decided they needed a comedic element for the show. Young, thin, brash television comic Johnny Carson was summoned and quickly flew to England to participate in the special; neither an unsuspecting Anka nor Carson realized then that they would eventually collaborate on an effort that would make millionaires of them.

"I ran into him again in New York after that," Anka says. "Coincidentally, his managers had an office in the same building as my accountant. We started discussing things and he told me he was contemplating taking over *The Tonight Show* and changing this and changing that.

"We discussed the music and sat down, and I said, 'Let me write a theme for you.'"

Anka did. Soon after their meeting, he sat down at a piano and plunked out a melody "that I thought would be fitting," Anka says confidently. "I think I knocked it off in one day." Then he sent, by messenger, a demo tape along with a lead sheet to Skitch Henderson at *The Tonight Show*; Henderson passed out the music to the members of the band for a trial run and further orchestration.

Johnny Carson listened intently to Anka's music. He smiled and enjoyed the theme. When the host debuted in the fall of 1962, so did "Johnny's Theme," which bore the names of both Anka and Carson on its sheet music as cowriters. At that time, Carson was slightly nervous about following Jack Paar, and felt a responsibility to oversee most elements of his new show, which he really wanted to succeed.

"Actually, *I* wrote it," Anka admits, "but when we talked about it, I got certain attitudes . . . or suggestions from him along with his input, so I put him on as cowriter."

Fate was good to Anka then, as it has been many times in his prolific career as a songwriter and singer. "Johnny's Theme" is not unlike his Academy Award–nominated score for the film *The Longest Day*; both musical milestones evolved from a simple inquiry.

**Paul Anka, the singer and songwriter who gave us "My Way" and "Puppy Love," made "Johnny's Theme" one of the most recognized tunes in television. *(courtesy of Paul Anka)***

"Johnny's Theme" is the only song written by Anka that lacks lyrics. It's been a consistent money-maker for Anka, who has cumulatively garnered "in excess of a million dollars" from it, he reports. Based on BMI's formula for payment, which has fluctuated over the years, he's estimated the song has produced an annual income of "between fifty and seventy-five thousand a year." In a rare interview with Bob Costas on NBC's *Later*, Anka jokingly said the television theme "put a few kids through college."

He confirms the tune's educational value as humorous but realistic. "Really, it's true if you think about it," he says.

Anka is quick to say he's "a big Johnny Carson fan," watching the late-night show as often as possible. He's only appeared a half-dozen times, but that's the way he wants it. After his hearing the song night after night, week after week, for three decades, if he were less than enthusiastic about hearing it once again live, it would be no wonder. But, he says, he's not tired of it at all. "Are you kidding?" he says twice. To Anka it's a sweet sound that he'll probably miss when Johnny, and the song, retire.

Wisely, successor Jay Leno plans to revamp *The Tonight Show*, which means introducing a new theme song. Carson is as instantly associated with Anka's recognizable ditty as Bob Hope is with "Thanks for the Memory." And who else but the Great One could part a curtain and step out to the tune of "Melancholy Serenade"? So, for Carson, "Johnny's Theme" is a signature tune that America won't forget or disassociate from him, possibly ever.

"It's so recognizable to the public despite the fact that they hear it each night for such a short time," Anka ponders. "What—maybe ten, fifteen, thirty seconds at the most each night? But everybody knows it. Simplicity is indeed royal."

Over the years, "Johnny's Theme" has remained just that: Johnny's. Used almost exclusively by Carson, except in live appearances by Doc Severinsen and a few members of *The Tonight Show* orchestra who have strayed for an out-of-town gig, the theme has not been altered through the decades. Its fame is not derived from any personal plugs by its creator, nor is it featured during Paul Anka concerts.

"I make light mention of it during concerts," he says, "but I don't really address it at any other time. Its usage comes up more orally from people. I've never recorded it or promoted it or changed it. That may be a paradox—something as important as that, I think."

Anka has plenty of other tunes to play with during his sellout appearances across the country or more likely in Las Vegas. He gave us "My Way" most popularly recorded by ol' Blue Eyes. He also wrote "Puppy Love" for Mouseketeer Annette Funicello, although most would probably recall Donny Osmond's version. Songs such as "Having My Baby," "You Are My Destiny," and "Lonely Boy," among nearly six hundred others are credited to his discography. His work has been recorded by the best: Sinatra, Streisand, Buddy Holly, Tom Jones, Connie Francis, Elvis Presley. Sid Vicious is in there somewhere, too.

Along the way, Anka has built an empire with some forty hit singles, eighteen gold records, and sales that have reached 100 million. And of all the tunes he's penned, one of his most successful, and most recognized, is one he's never recorded for release—and one to which he attached not a single word. Anka's recently been toying with that thought.

"I've contemplated maybe somewhere near the ending broadcast to come on [*The Tonight Show*] doing a special lyric using that melody," he says. "And dedicate the song to Johnny. I'd like to do that."

# Memorable Moments

## The Marriage of Tiny Tim

Perhaps the highest rated *Tonight Show* ever is a genuine enigma. It was a highly touted evening of wedded bliss between novelty performer Tiny Tim, real name Herbert Buckingham Khaury, and his seventeen-year-old fiancée, Miss Vicki, real name Victoria May Budinger. The ninety-minute show on December 17, 1969, started as usual with Johnny's monologue (peppered with wedding and honeymoon jokes), and the guests included Phyllis Diller and Florence Henderson. The fifteen-minute marriage at the tail end of the show, however, was the center of attention and grabbed an astronomical 85 percent share—whopping by any standards. To this day, program directors, who grind their teeth nights dreaming of hits, ask themselves why.

Talent coordinator Craig Tennis was the young staffer responsible for booking Tiny Tim to Carson shows long before the televised-wedding concept had ever been formulated. Says Tennis, "Just having him walk through the office on his visit—a white-faced Baby Huey with the shopping bag and the ukulele neck sticking out of it and his mincing little gait—was enough to send everybody in the offices into shock, and enough to make me feel a little leery, too."

Tennis said booking Tiny Tim on *The Tonight Show* was a risk. It would "either go down as the most disastrous moment in ten years of broadcasting on *The Tonight Show,* or it would score as something monumental." No one had any idea of the eventual landmark Tiny Tim would create. No one knew why he was on the show.

To Carson as well as audiences across the nation, the sight of this tall, awkward man with a hawk nose, falsetto singing voice, long, curly jet-black hair, plucking a ukulele and singing "Tiptoe Through the Tulips" was beyond comprehension. Was he the sixties or the twenties? Was he a genius or a fool? Was he talented or was he just silly? On Carson's couch, he was the kid in school who always had his homework. He was shy, dainty, and he spoke in a soft, Michael Jacksonesque voice, covering his mouth like a schoolgirl when he giggled. Imagine Boy George, only 1969. Carson always played it straight, never berating his guest. Imagine David Letterman interviewing Tiny Tim. Don Rickles might have torn Tiny Tim into tiny pieces.

On another appearance, Tiny Tim sang "Living in the Sunlight, Loving in the Moonlight," a catchy little tune made famous by Maurice Chevalier in 1929. "You don't do it like Chevalier," Carson quipped rhetorically. Audiences erupted as Carson's innocent

*The televised marriage of Tiny Tim and Miss Vicki remained the highest rated Tonight Show, predictably to be topped by Johnny's final night as host. (Personality Photos, Inc.)*

facial expressions—a mixture of bewilderment and embarrassment, pure Nebraska—
told the story. Carson was on the verge of hilarity.

After several appearances, the wild idea of airing Tiny Tim's wedding on the show
developed. Carson asked Tiny if he'd like the ceremony to take place right on the show,
and Tiny's hands fluttered as he shot back, "Oh, could we?"

*The* wedding to see on national television was advertised heavily, and the prenup-
tial publicity was not in vain. None of the 268 studio tickets were disbursed to the public; only invited guests of the bride and groom got seats.

"Tiny Tim must have requested me," guest Phyllis Diller says. Diller, of course, is
known for her wild wardrobe. "I remember distinctly I was in New York doing *Hello,
Dolly!* on Broadway. I said 'No, I can't make the show,' because they taped at five-thirty, and in the theater, you have to be there a half hour before curtain. I didn't see how I
could possibly manage with New York traffic, even then.

"Honey, they sent a police escort. By then I was so confused, I had forgotten that at
the wedding, everyone was to be formal, *including* the crew. I arrived in a short, shiny
dress, and Shirley Wood, the talent coordinator, took her long purple wool dress off,
and I put it on."

Hordes of press inquired about the sanctity of the ceremony, but NBC and the
*Tonight Show* staff insisted there would be no toying with this legal marriage. Critic
Jack Miller of the *Ontario Spectator* noted, "If Tiny himself wants to make a sideshow
of this, that's his business—and there remains the suspicion that he's the biggest put-
on to hit the U.S. since those Japanese peace delegates in 1941."

Nonetheless, a gamut of press swarmed the studio that evening to cover the best-
attended wedding of the year. Perhaps it was the most witnessed wedding ever.

Preparations for the event were detailed: ten thousand tulips were provided by Ab-
erdeen's Flowers of Chicago. The seven-foot wedding cake, prepared by a Wilmington,
Delaware, bakery, was on display a day before it arrived at the studio in New York. The
bride wore a twenty-five-hundred-dollar Victorian gown, the groom a black silk velvet
frock coat with top hat and cane.

The ceremony began with "I, Tiny Tim, being of sound mind . . ." The Reverend
William Glenesk presided while Johnny, Ed, and guests, all decked in formal attire,
watched. After the ceremony, which was applauded by the audience, Tiny Tim prepared milk and honey for him and his bride to toast, while Johnny broke open a bottle
of champagne. Naturally, Ed was nearby to partake. Then Tiny sang two songs to his
bride. The first one was titled "The Wedding Song for Miss Vicki." In his high-pitched
vocals, he sang:

> *"Oh won't you come and love me, O pretty Vicki mine,*
> *Oh won't you come and love me, and be my valentine,*
> *Like violets and roses, our spirits will entwine,*
> *Like violets and roses, our bodies will combine."*

Then he sang another tune, "You Were There." Singer Nick Lukas, who recorded "Tiptoe Through the Tulips" in the 1929 film *Gold Diggers of Broadway*, was flown in to
reprise *his* song, which eventually became the trademark for Tiny Tim. Rudy Vallee, star
of the *Gold Diggers* film, was scheduled to be a guest at Tiny's request, but was a no-show.

The press reported the wedding kiss was "the couple's third osculatory contact," and that after the wedding Tiny and Miss Vicki planned to observe three days of abstinence, which derived from the prophet Tobias in the Old Testament. Said Tiny: "Not even a kiss. I plan to give the Lord the first fruits of my marriage. If only more people followed the ways of Saint Paul and King David."

Although millions of viewers attested to this union, its destiny seemed doomed almost immediately. Weeks after the show, the minister who married the odd couple sued the producers of *The Tonight Show* for five hundred dollars. The Reverend William Glenesk, acting as his own attorney in Brooklyn Small Claims Court, filed the suit, saying producer Rudy Tellez promised him the usual $265 appearance fee but also said he would pay Glenesk's membership fee into the American Federation of Television and Radio Artists with another invitation to appear on *The Tonight Show* attached. Tellez denied the promises, and later the suit was settled. Outside the courtroom, the minister explained why he was pressing for additional money. "I had to make a serious ceremony in a circus situation before thirty million people," he said. "And that's hard work."

Tiny Tim blended milk and honey for himself and his bride, after the marriage ceremony that took place on *The Tonight Show*. Johnny and Ed broke uncorked champagne. *(Personality Photos, Inc.)*

Alas, the marriage of Tiny and Vicki ended in divorce in 1977, an end sought by Vicki. But by then, one of the most bizarre events on television was already written into the history books. Tiny Tim still tours the country, records songs, and plucks the ukulele in his unusual act that has attracted a cult following.

Answering the obvious question of the event, one writer put it: "Not only was the fluttery, silver-voiced tenor getting married to a girl (which looked highly unlikely) but everything was done for maximum attention." Phyllis Diller simply states: "Tiny Tim was at his peak in 1969. And we're talking about a freak. I know he will never be on that show again. I saw a recent appearance, and what he did he would have been pegged as [the acts of] a crazy person.

"He gained about eight hundred pounds, you know. He sang, and during the number, he simply fell to the floor and you could see his bare stomach while he writhed on the floor during the song. Tiptoeing is one thing. Writhing is another."

## Michael Landon

Johnny Carson fidgeted more than usual. His forehead tight with tension, he nervously introduced the next guest:

"I think most of the nation and the world probably know by now that on April eighth, Michael Landon was diagnosed as having inoperable cancer of the pancreas and liver, and that would stun everybo—anybody. But like Michael Landon, he met the problem head-on. He invited the press to his house and told them the situation. He did that mainly to avoid the rumors, the speculation, the misinformation; and to try to avoid sensationalism by the tabloids. And for the past month, he has continued to face this battle with humor, honesty, and a personal sense of dignity that characterizes the man. Would you welcome . . . Michael Landon. . . ."

History was in the making as Landon walked jauntily out from the curtain, obviously ready both physically and mentally for his appearance. The camera panned the audience as the crowd stood to welcome the actor with a warm round of applause. He hugged Johnny, moved around the desk, and hugged Ed. The studio audience was packed, leaving a trail of hopefuls outside NBC; some were crying because they did not get in.

Landon's ovation continued until the actor raised a hand to halt the applause. This would prove to be his last public appearance.

He was wearing a bright turquoise shirt with light beige pants—the same colors he wore on April 8, nearly a month prior, when he summoned the press to his home to an-

**Michael Landon jokes with pal Johnny Carson in the early seventies. Landon's final appearance in 1991, just weeks before his death of cancer, was the second-highest-rated** *Tonight Show* **ever.** *(Personality Photos, Inc.)*

nounce to the world that he had been diagnosed with cancer. He looked thin, especially along his actor's jaw, but kept his brows raised. He looked tired but retained his humor.

Landon was the veteran of numerous appearances with Carson, his neighbor in Malibu and tennis buddy from way back. Carson enjoyed Landon's career, and mutually, Landon professed to never miss a *Tonight Show* when his pal was hosting. He had carte blanche to appear on the program, and the pair were said to be seen chumming around town frequently.

Carson mused about the time the two were dining at the trendy Beaurivage restaurant in Malibu, when Landon cunningly convinced him that he had backed over the restaurant owner's cat in the parking lot. Carson didn't want to return to the eatery a month later, but Landon insisted.

Carson had arranged for the waiter to serve a nice dish with a fake flattened cat on a silver platter. Landon was one-up. When the two arrived, specially designed menus were offered with entrées stylishly listed in old English calligraphy, fancy and believable. As Carson perused the menu with Landon sitting across the table, he noticed unusual dishes like Tureen of Tabby . . . $8.75 (served with scallions, tomatoes, cucumbers . . . in 30-weight oil) . . . Baked Fillet of Feline.

"I go to the next page and I see 'Pussy Mousse à la Mercedes . . . prepared right on the property,'" Carson says, laughing. "And then I get down to this one here . . . 'Pressed Pussy Provençale' . . . served outside in the dark.'"

Trying to keep the mood light, Carson joked as usual with his guest, also aware that it might be one of the last times he'd see his friend. Since Landon's illness had been made public, every show on the air pined for his presence. Barbara Walters called requesting an interview, as did the *60 Minutes* people and many others. Harry Flynn, a spokesman for Landon, was quoted in the *Hollywood Reporter* about the scheduled appearance: "He wanted to go somewhere where he could show people he isn't all that sick. . . . He wants people to know he's hanging in there despite the deathbed stories appearing in the tabs. He wanted to go on a show and lighten up. It will not be maudlin. It will be fun."

Carson said he was flattered to make room for Landon on the night he wished, May 9, 1991. The primary reason Landon mustered the strength, dyed his roots, and asked his pal permission to stop by the show once again was to publicly reprimand the tabloids that had exploited his illness. One tabloid had issued a dictum declaring he had four weeks to live. The *National Enquirer* led its front page with glaring bold letters: MICHAEL LANDON: IT'S OVER! Such screaming sensationalism frightened his family and angered the actor. Overtly stern, he turned to the audience at one point and said, "It's unbelievable that people can be that way. That's the cancer you know. That's the cancer in our society."

Carson responded: "I think that most people watching with a scintilla of intelligence realize that most of those things like the *Enquirer*, and the *Star* . . . are garbage."

Landon also wished to clear up what he called "this tenth-child business." Setting up a punch line, he said, "There's a big headline in one of those incredible tabloid magazines about the fact that I want to have a tenth child so my wife will have something to remember me by. Here I've got nine kids, nine dogs, three grandkids—one in the oven—three parrots . . . and my wife, Cindy, needs something to remember me by?"

The atmosphere was tense and almost silent in the beginning, and Carson himself was ill at ease about the show. Backstage, Cindy and a few of the Landon children sat in special seats to watch the show, while all of Studio One was under heavy surveillance curtailing press attempts to snap a shot of the actor. Reportedly, there was an open offer from a tabloid for fifty thousand dollars to anyone who could snap a shot of Landon at the studio or in his dressing room. Hours before the taping, photographers outside NBC's guest entrance converged on each limousine braking to enter, snapping shots into the windows not knowing who was inside.

Later, onstage, almost immediately after Landon joined Carson, the tension eased as the ailing actor joked and laughed with hearty strength. Throughout the show, he exuded optimism and emphasized the importance of high spirits in handling disease. "I just want to say one thing," Landon said seriously. "For any of those families out there who have a relative who has cancer . . . They know how tough the fight is and how important the mental attitude is . . . and how you pull together and keep a very, very up attitude. Mentally, it's more than fifty percent of your medicine."

Before cameras, the two friends discussed the illness, the press, and even the proposed cures that came in bagfuls to the Landon residence. One involved coffee enemas, which Landon admitted trying. "I invited John over for a coffee enema, but he wanted cream and sugar and I'm not pourin'!" he joked. Carson quipped: "You better make sure somebody hasn't secretly replaced your coffee with Folger's Crystals . . . or it could be a long day."

Landon continued: "I really want to thank everybody. [I've received] a lot of great suggestions, and I'm using a little bit of everything.

"Although"—he grinned—"there were some I didn't try. One guy wrote me and told me that the reason I got the Big C was that I did not get enough sex. See, he thinks it was only the nine times when I had the kids . . . well, he gave me this regimen which would kill the average twenty-five-year-old.

"I've gotten tapes, books, you name it," Landon continued. "Swim with a dolphin. You only have to do it once. Something about sonar from the dolphin and—ping-ping!—it goes away. What can I tell you? Here I'm goin' to all these hospitals, and I only gotta go to Marineland!"

Landon rested on the couch while the next guest, fighter George Foreman, came to the platform and joked with Carson until the end of the show. After the taping was completed, Carson hugged Landon, and the crowd was hesitant to leave its seats. The audience clapped and rose for the stricken actor as he waved, said "Bye," and walked behind the curtain.

Watching the show closely, Joseph Wallison, the brother of George Foreman's attorney, accompanied the fighter to the studio. He had been backstage before, but tonight he wanted an autograph from both Carson and Landon.

"Backstage it was quiet through the whole show, and everybody seemed on edge," Wallison says. "The tension was so thick . . . like they were scared to have him on the show. Here's a guy with a matter of weeks to live, and they're putting him on TV."

Landon laughed in his dressing room, next to Foreman's, and the two joked about sports and Landon's record as a champion javelin thrower. Brandon Tartikoff, head of NBC, was also backstage waiting to speak with Landon. Most of the crew and NBC pages knew they should not bother the actor, so Landon was left relatively to himself and his manager. Meantime, Wallison searched for Johnny Carson to ask for his signature, but the host was noticeably absent until curtain time. Everyone said Johnny was "uptight."

"Michael Landon was cool as a cucumber, like nothing was wrong," observed Wallison. "He was positive, friendly. After the show, he went and hugged friends and family backstage. Security was attempting to rush him out, and I had to practically walk in between security guys and him to shove a picture in his face and ask for an autograph."

Wallison was prepared with a black Sharpie marker pen and a color eight-by-ten-inch publicity still from *Highway to Heaven* showing a peaceful Landon gazing into the clouded sky. He brought another, but the security guard warned, "Only one."

"I told him I was a big fan and asked him if he would sign the picture for me, and he said, 'Sure.'" Wallison says. "I patted him on the back and said, 'Thanks.' He looked healthy, like he had just lost weight. Not much makeup on him. Then they escorted him back to his dressing room, and Carson was nowhere to be found."

Wallison later speculated he might have been handed Landon's final autograph.

Landon nearly doubled the ratings that night. Nielsen Ratings Services reported the appearance scored a 10.4 rating, which translates to a 24 percent audience share in its twenty-five major markets, easily winning the time slot. It was the highest overnight rating for a *Tonight* in recent memory, claimed an NBC official. Each overnight ratings point equaled 446,215 homes. Translated, this meant that it was the highest-rated segment in the past ten years, and the second-highest-rated since Carson assumed the hosting position in 1962. Landon told his wife, Cindy, that he was pleased America was watching.

On Monday, July 1, 1991, Michael Landon, at age fifty-four, died at his home in Malibu, with his family around him.

Johnny Carson released a statement about his longtime friend: "This has been a devastating week for me and my family. Michael called last Monday expressing his deepest sympathy on the death of my son, Ricky. The courage and sensitivity he showed in our conversation, in comforting me while he was in great pain, attests to the quality of this man and his character."

## More Memorable Moments . . .

Probably the excerpt that has gotten the most mileage in *Tonight Show* anniversary specials is the famous Ed Ames tomahawk-throw from 1965.

Ames, a costar in the TV series *Daniel Boone* as Mingo the Indian, was demonstrating the art of tossing a tomahawk at the preferred point on a large wooden silhouette of a human figure. Ames joked at first, quickly took aim, and "plunk," the tomahawk landed directly in the crotch of the wooden dummy. Ames, laughing, claimed it was a mistake, and Carson wouldn't let him hide his embarrassment by exiting backstage. He grabbed his arm for a few more jokes with the audience, which was laughing wildly. "I didn't even know you were Jewish," Carson quipped. (This episode had been parodied on *Saturday Night Live.* Dan Aykroyd, as Ames, hacked away at the silhouette's crotch until it was kindling. It was a sarcastic comment on the overused warhorse clip from Classic Carson archives).

- Remember the night when actor Oliver Reed was making some strong comments about the "place" of women in the home? Shelley Winters, a previous guest on the show, had suddenly exited the platform while Reed was talking to Johnny.

  > REED: *I think a woman's place is looking after her man and children. . . .*
  > *I think the man's place is to look after her, protect her, and pro-*
  > *vide her with a little warmth.*
  > CARSON: *The old-fashioned concept, huh?*

  Just then, someone made a comment from the audience, and Reed looked up and said, "Shhhh! Quiet, woman!" Shelley Winters reappeared on the scene with a full glass of water, walked up in front of Reed, and poured the water over his head. She walked off the set, and the audience was in hysterics. Reed just sat there.

- Ed McMahon spoke of his Alpo days on *The Tonight Show*, when he delivered the "live" commercials during the breaks. He told host Bob Costas on TV's *Later*:

  > *I had this dog that was so great. . . . His name was Patrick. He was an*
  > *English sheepdog and had those white, furry eyes. He was so in tune*
  > *with what he was doing. He was Mr. Show Business. He would sleep*
  > *in between the seats in Studio 6B on the concrete where it was cool.*
  > *When he heard my voice in the back of the studio, he stood up and*
  > *walked to the commercial area because he knew we were gonna re-*
  > *hearse. I had a small amount of Alpo in the bowl, and I'd put it down*
  > *and do the spiel for a minute.*
  >
  > *One night, for some reason, when I put the Alpo down, he came in,*
  > *took one smell of the Alpo, and walked out. Here I am. I've got a bowl*
  > *of Alpo. One minute and no dog. Johnny, bless him, comes in on all*
  > *fours and pretends to eat the food, and lick my leg.*

- The biggest, brightest stars have shined on *The Tonight Show*, over the years. Some have refused, like Cary Grant, Britain's Benny Hill, and Jack Nicholson. Some may recall the bearded, large actor Victor Buono when he eloquently delivered hilarious narrations of his writings like Shakespeare-gone-bad. Others may remember a few classic character actors stopping by, like the tall, balding, everlasting octogenarian Burt Mustin (Gus on *Leave It to Beaver*), who came on the show January 15, 1976, not long before his death. You may recall one of the last public appearances of character actor William Demarest, who came out wearing a nice sweater and had that thin red hair perfectly slicked just like his famous persona Uncle Charlie on *My Three Sons*.

- Baseball great Pete Rose emerged from the curtain in a rare interview in 1991 after he had been imprisoned for gambling on the sport that made him famous. Rose said first thing, "Nice to be here . . . and Doc, thanks for not playin' 'Jailhouse Rock.'" Then he told Johnny this was his first appearance on the show: "All these [baseball] records I got. . . . You gotta go to prison to get on this show!"

- One classy night in 1984 on *The Tonight Show*, the Great One, Jackie Gleason, made his first appearance on the show while in Hollywood filming what became his last movie, *Nothing in Common*, with Tom Hanks. Natty as usual, Gleason came out in a tailored light gray suit, red carnation, cuff links, and a diamond pinkie ring. The comic genius of television (Gleason, that is) smoked seven cigarettes during the extended interview, while subjects such as *The Honeymooners*, aspects of comedy, and "drinking" were approached.

  Gleason said: "I'm not advocating that everybody should drink—it just worked for me. And of course the gentleman on my right [McMahon] has had a taste or two."

  Gleason was a bit shaky at the time, unknowingly suffering from cancer, and exited with a gracious kiss and wave to the audience while the band played his *Honeymooners* theme. Most of us expected his "And a-waaaaay we go!" cartoonlike exit.

  Carson, who emulates Gleason frequently, concluded: "He's remarkable. . . . That gentleman has never received an Emmy, if you can believe it, from the Television Academy in this business. And the Academy ought to be towed out twenty miles and dropped in the ocean. Something's wrong there."

- Charlton Heston was on one evening in the 1970s with Johnny; the two thought they'd treat the audience to some "classical" orations, both standing at podiums. Stately postured, they read from their souls.

  HESTON:    *There was a young lady of Norway*
  *Who hung by her toes in the doorway.*
  *She said to her beau, "Hey look at me, Joe!*
  *I think I've discovered one more way."*

  CARSON:    *There was an old preacher named Spencer*
  *Whose abstinence made him grow tenser.*
  *So he called up a chick, who came over real quick,*
  *For the rest you better check with the censor.*

  HESTON:    *There was a young man with a hernia,*
  *Who said to his Dr. Galdernia,*
  *"When improving my middle,*
  *Be sure not to fiddle*
  *With matters that do not concern ya."*

- During a commercial for a cellophane wrap, Ed McMahon was supposed to demonstrate its sealing ability by applying a piece over a wine goblet filled with wine and turning it upside down. No wine was supposed to leak out.

  "I did something wrong, and I overlapped a piece of it or something," says McMahon, "because when I turned it over, the wine leaked out. . . .

  "Here the commercial is blown, and it's all over for the sponsor. The audience is laughing, and I'm making a fool of myself. So I took a chance. I walked out front and over to the desk with another glass of wine. Put it down, took the wrap, and put it on the glass. I sealed it very carefully this time and turned it upside down over Johnny's head. Thank God nothing dripped out. It could've been the end of a nice career."

# The Grand Couple of *The Tonight Show*

As I approached them for this interview, I sent a scribbled note across the aisle and down a few rows: *Hello. My name is Steve Cox. I'm writing a book about* The Tonight Show *and I've heard you've been to MANY. I've heard a lot about you. May I speak to you after the show? . . . Steve Cox. P.S. Look behind you.*

Betty and Bob stood up as if Studio One were their living room, and waved with a huge grin. "Sure!" They nodded.

Betty and Bob Kelly are like the grand couple of *The Tonight Show.* She's sixty-nine and he's seventy, and in their retirement they enjoy one thing together: Studio One, doesn't matter if it's Jay or Johnny or Joan. They've seen 'em all and say they will continue to see them.

Betty and Bob have seen close to eight hundred *Tonight Shows* live in Burbank. Sammy Davis , Jr., was their favorite singer on the show, "by far." They brave heat and rain and wait in line for hours like everyone else to get in. They're the first to clap during the warm-up. Carson sees them in the front row almost every night, but they've never met their "Johnny."

"Some people think we're crazy, coming and standing in line," says Bob Kelly, a retired manager of a ware-housing company. He looks a bit like Bert Lahr, with a pleasant laugh to match. Betty sparks a familiar, gentle gid-diness . . . sort of like Edith Bunker. "It's a different show every night. Different guests, different music," Bob professes. "If you've seen the show here, you know the music is good."

Betty's favorite routine is Floyd Turbo. Bob says he can't decide. They remember one particular show from which a woman with a knife was carted away by Security. Holidays prompt NBC to lay out a buffet spread in the lobby for the audience, they say. Pictures prove they met Jay Leno tanking up one of his classic cars at the gas sta-tion across the street. But they've never met Johnny.

"One of the crew got his autograph on this picture," says Betty as she points to a color still signed to both of them. Nothing special in the message, but it's definitely Carson's signature.

"We've always known he's a private person, so you don't go flag him down," Betty says. In a scrapbook, they've assembled odds and ends from shows: tickets, photos, autographs, articles, dates, notes, and mementos from NBC. One piece of paper is signed by the whole *Tonight Show* band.

"There was another fellow who used to come here and we had figured out that he had seen something like twenty-five hundred shows," Bob says. "For fourteen years, he came every night! Dunno what happened to him."

Of their stops at NBC each morning to pick up tickets and their later wait in line that afternoon, they reminisce that Michael Landon's last appearance was the most tense. Barry Manilow and Julio Iglesias both have fan clubs that camp out in line overnight to catch appearances, they explain. And they've stumbled across some rude, im-patient first-timers who jump the line. They've never played "Stump the Band" because they can't sing.

"Those people are always picked out ahead of time," Bob explains. "Johnny knows where they are sitting. We're a wealth of information," he laughs. Because they are first in line, most first-timers ask the Kellys questions. The NBC pages have almost counted on their good-natured assistance in handling the crowds before the doors are officially opened. Once they are, it's "Hi Betty! Hi Bob! How's your day goin'? Oh, I brought some pictures to show you. . . ." The pages are like grandchildren, and Betty bakes cookies for them occasionally.

They watch the show in the evening on television most nights as well. Sometimes they see themselves, but they are not particularly enthusiastic about that, they say. Watching *The Tonight Show* taped each afternoon, they

**Betty and Bob Kelly, regulars to Studio One at NBC, have attended nearly eight hundred shows.** *(photo by Stephen Cox)*

say, is a life they find enjoyable and relaxing. They say they know good entertainment, "so why pay tickets to see concerts when it's free 'most every week?" Bob asks.

Although Betty and Bob Kelly enjoy Jay Leno, they're going to miss their Johnny, they say. They're used to him, like everyone else . . . only just a few feet closer.

# 3

# Celebrities on *Tonight*

## Tony Randall

It could be a play, a film, a TV series, a charity event. Or maybe the book he wrote (*Which Reminds Me,* published by Delacorte Press, he informs me). But Tony Randall realizes an appearance with Johnny Carson means business.

"I'm always on the show to plug something," Randall admits. "That's the reason to go on. It's Plugsville. I've never gone on except to plug something. That's why people go on for no money. It's the finest avenue there is to advertise something."

Although he seems to have escaped the aging process the same way Dick Clark has, Randall has been in television since the medium's infancy. He costarred in TV's *Mr. Peepers* with Wally Cox when sitcoms aired live from New York, and he hasn't stopped yet. His most recent appearance on *The Tonight Show* prompted Carson to introduce him saying, "This is a big night for us . . . Tony Randall's millionth appearance. . . ." Randall doesn't care, because he's admittedly up-front about it all. His position in most facets of the entertainment business, especially television, is secure. His wit is sharp, which explains his open invitation to the Carson show.

On more than 125 occasions, Randall has stepped from the curtain, usually as huckster for some personal cause. Each time he is more nervous.

"And I'm *never* nervous," he professes. "I don't have *any* stage fright. *None.* Opening night I can go to sleep in my dressing room until ten minutes before my entrance. I'm blessed that way. But I'm *always* nervous before Carson."

It's due to his record of success with Carson, he says. Every appearance has been a good one. Not a sour show in the bundle. "I keep thinking, sooner or later we've got to bomb. Am I going to be funny tonight? I guess that's a comedian's fear."

The producers and Carson agree that Tony Randall is a good guest, at least on *The Tonight Show*. Plug or no plug, Randall's conversation is amusing. And his aim is perfect when he explains the target nature of television as a touting tool.

"Before television got this big, if you had a movie, a play, a book, a record—the most you could hope for or the greatest thing that could happen was to get the cover of *LIFE* magazine," Randall says. "That would sell. Today, it's television, and above all, Johnny Carson. If you look at it any other way, you're misconstruing it."

Still, today Randall eagerly and consistently plugs not a tangible thing or an item for purchase, but a notion: Stop Smoking. He's said it many times on *The Tonight Show* and for Carson, who's smoked for years, it eventually became a running gag. While Ran-

ODD COUPLE: Tony Randall told Carson in 1977 of his ailment known as tinnitus, in which he suffers constant ringing in his ears. It was so loud, Randall said, that Johnny might be able to hear it. "I can," Carson quipped. *(courtesy of Tony Randall)*

On the show one evening were Helen and Frank Beardsley, parents of twenty children. Johnny asked, "How do you manage, having twenty children?" Mrs. Beardsley replied, "I'm doing what I enjoy most. . . . I guess I was just made for it."

The audience, and Carson, broke up. After they left, Johnny said, "I only
have three children, I don't know how they do it." A member of the audience
yelled, "Oh yes you do!"

dall sat there, smoke would eventually waft his way. Carson and Randall got a lot of
mileage out of the joke; Randall would rant like his Felix Unger character from the Neil
Simon sitcom. (*The Odd Couple*, ABC-TV; 1970–75; "Continually run in syndication," he
adds.)

Carson respects the notion, though. During the 1960s, he openly puffed away, leaving a lit cigarette balanced on the edge of a glass ashtray on the desk. It was nothing
for him to take a drag while interviewing someone, or pinch out the flame while delivering a funny retort to a guest. Today, he's adamant about not smoking on-camera, although a little ashtray sits beside him, where props, little items, and a pitcher of water
are invisibly present. These days, he also doesn't allow staff photographers to snap him
with a cigarette in his mouth or with one wedged between his fingers.

"I think every now and then he quits," says Randall, who is openly bothered by
smoke—and equally vocal about it. "When I'd come on, he'd light up without a word,
knowing that I'd say something. He provokes you, and it's so sly.

"You see, it's misdirection. He was a magician once; you're watching his left hand,
but his right hand's doing it."

Conversations with Randall have swayed, believe it or not, from personal plugs to
other entertaining topics, all gracefully facilitated by Carson. Once, Randall remembers fondly, singer Carmen Lombardo was on the show, and Randall, who imitates
Lombardo singing "Boo Hoo," was pitted against the singer in an impromptu "Boo Hoo"
competition. Carson gauged the audience's reaction by a hand-over-the-head applause
meter. Randall saved that episode on videotape, a rarity, since he detests watching
himself on television.

On another memorable show, Randall discussed his longtime physical ailment
called tinnitus, which causes the sufferer to constantly detect ringing in the inner ear.

"That show had remarkable consequences," he says. "I told him I had tinnitus and
I'd gone to doctors and tried everything. There is no cure. Every doctor had said the
same thing to me: Learn to live with it.

"I got hundreds of letters saying, 'You claim you've cured your tinnitus. . . . How did
you do it?'" he says. "People don't listen. The American Tinnitus Foundation asked me
to come aboard, and I've been active with them ever since." (American Tinnitus Association, Box 5, Portland, Oregon 97207)

One more plug, Randall interrupts. This time, it's for Johnny Carson. Remember,
Tony Randall believes in his convictions and eloquently expresses exactly what he

thinks. "I sit there with my mouth gaping," Randall says of his television appearances with Carson. "And every time, when the show's over, I say the same thing to him: 'Johnny, you're the most brilliant man in the world.' It seems to embarrass him. I don't think he likes it.

"I remember Kenneth Tynan wrote that Johnny Carson was an authentic genius, and I've quoted that a number of times," says Randall of the late critic from *The New Yorker*. "He's an authentic comic genius, and people should recognize that."

## Buddy Hackett

Unbeknownst to the viewing audience, while Middle America is waiting through pizza commercials or spots for new cars, the studio audience at NBC is witnessing an earful of Buddy Hackett telling an off-color story with his usual candor. It's one of the few times that a guest at the couch interacts with the audience during a commercial break, and the band is stifled, also listening to Hackett. When Johnny returns from a commercial, Hackett usually re-starts the story, only for Johnny to nervously cut him off for fear of certain words. "Why don't you let me send you out into the world," Hackett pleads, with a blue joke on the tip of his tongue. "'Cause I'll say somethin' and . . ." Immediately, Johnny changes the subject.

**Buddy Hackett, known for keeping Carson on the edge with his provocative jokes, is one of the host's favorite visitors to the show.** *(courtesy of Buddy Hackett)*

"I walk along the edge so carefully, the audience is with bated breath thinkin', How is he gonna get out of this one?" Hackett says, describing his usual *Tonight Show* fare. If you're not a Buddy Hackett follower, or you haven't seen any of his concert appearances, the stories he tells are usually blue—maybe intense violet. But they are never forced with random cursing to shock an audience like the tactic some comics employ. Each word of Hackett's delivery is carefully planned, distinctly delivered, and funny. Mostly, sex is the target he chooses on *The Tonight Show.* But what's new? The same innuendos surface with Carson's conversation, maybe not quite as direct, and not in such a detailed story filled with dialects and perfectly timed gestures.

"[Buddy's] possibly the funniest man of all," says Fred de Cordova, of the guests who stop by the show. "He's very risqué in all other venues but very circumspect with us, except during the commercials when we're off the air. Johnny enjoys him as much as the audience does."

Over the years, Hackett has fine-tuned his appearances, although it's not beneath him to impulsively start removing his clothes just out of the camera's range while Ed McMahon is doing an Alpo commercial, such as one fine evening. Any "Hackett night" on the show is usually not for plugging—just playful jokes and ad-libbing with Johnny. That doesn't mean, however, he has not utilized that strength of the medium to his advantage. "You can go on any part of episodic television and play a great part and get nominated and such," he says, "but that won't bring one person to see you in a nightclub. Every time I went on his show to plug an upcoming appearance, it was sold out. The same people who stay up to eleven-thirty to see John, these are the same people who go to nightclubs and theater."

Hopefully, Hackett has time to sift through his mental joke file and come up with a few killers to spring on Johnny and the audience. Cracking up Johnny is the easily accessible object, and the rest seems to fall in place for him. "I'm only nervous *ahead* of time, trying to think of what stories to tell on the show," says the rotund raconteur. But when he's on, he's concentrating heavily on his performance, giving it his best for Johnny and the audience. He's not thinking of dinner that evening, or whether his fly is open. He starts the stories, and every ear in the studio is perked, listening intently. At least one tale in the bunch prompts Johnny to hop out of his seat, hysterically laughing out of embarrassment, and out of sheer humanness.

Before the show, there is a brief exchange or a brief "hello" between host and guest in the makeup room or the hallway. Never anything more. Spontaneity is the secret, Hackett explains. "One time I let him see me in the hall with a beautiful blue suit and a red tie," he says of a gag he pulled. "And Los Angeles had been going through such rain you couldn't believe it. As soon as he saw me, I went back to the dressing room, changed into a white suit with shoes and socks, and stood in the shower until I was soaked to the underwear.

"When he announced me, I walked out and said, 'It's still rainin', John!'"

Any other night you might catch the ever-tailored Hackett skirting off-color jokes, performing a little Three Stooges shtick with Johnny, or discussing a gig. The "weirdest" appearance he recalls was out of New York the night of an Academy Awards telecast.

"We had just started discussing the Awards as though they had already been on— but this was five-thirty, late afternoon," Hackett says, seriously. "We talked about which movies and which people won; it was just something I started, and John played along like nothing was up. We guessed *every one right*.

"After that, Price Waterhouse wanted to know how we had that information. Earl Wilson [syndicated columnist] came to my house and asked me how we got it. It was strange. We just guessed at it all and talked about it in the past tense, and it hadn't happened yet."

Carson calls Hackett one of the "self-starters" who come on the show wired and ready to entertain, leaving the spot open for a relatively effortless good time, because the guest is prepared. Hackett explains Carson's successful interview technique this way: "He is so brilliant. If he feels me needing something, he knows exactly what to say to bring it out of me. John makes every performer a star on his show, and I can't say enough about him. He's so utterly human. The only regret I ever have with John is that I don't see enough of him."

Reflecting on their friendship, Hackett recalls a few instances that meant most to him, which, not by coincidence, involve his pal Carson. "Of all the great times I've had," Hackett says, as if he's letting you in on a secret, "one night Johnny and I were together and went and watched comedians. We had a couple of drinks. Maybe more. But we laughed. He's one of the great laughers in the world. We went to see the burlesque comedians in Las Vegas. John fell out of his seat on the floor. Of all the nights I've spent in Las Vegas the last thirty-eight years, that was the best night after work I ever had."

Another highlight in Hackett's years was his birthday celebrated at the Candy Store in Los Angeles, when Johnny Carson was broadcasting from New York. It was a show night, and the Hacketts didn't feel Carson would be able to swing the trip in time, so an invitation was contemplated but not extended.

"It was maybe close to midnight, and the place was packed," Hackett remembers. "George Burns was there, Jack Benny was there, and everyone you could imagine. Johnny walks in. He walks right up to me and says, 'Who do you have to know to get invited to this party?' I was so thrilled he'd flown in, I couldn't even answer him. He said, 'Oh, you don't want me here?' I hugged him and kissed him.

"It was 1966 or '67, and about thirty people came to the house after the party. Jack Lemmon and his wife. Steve Allen. Nobody wanted to end the night. Johnny was sittin' on the floor with a pot, banging on the pot doing rhythms, you know. It was a wonderful night. And of all the birthdays I've had, that's one of my favorites. He made that night for me."

Hackett concluded: "So if you get an idea from this conversation that I'm a great Johnny Carson fan . . . I am."

# Phyllis Diller
## Carnac: Eleven
## Question: Bo Derek and Phyllis Diller

"There are some really funny things that Johnny's said about me that I adore," says the wacky comedienne, known for her own put-downs. "He was talking about a woman being raped. He said, 'Well, if it ever happened to Phyllis Diller, it would be breaking and entering.'"

By modern standards, the Diller style that stung America in the 1960s is mild. "I can't dress funny anymore," says the self-professed comic of the Geritol set. "They call it punk now. In vogue. Do you realize that spiked hairdo for five years was chic? Who do you think started that?"

In sync with the public or not, she admits, however, that she and Carson never managed magnetism at the desk and couch. On her last appearance with Carson, she performed a stand-up routine for the audience, a rarity for a comic

**Phyllis Diller, in a tame dress she hurriedly borrowed on the set, was present at the wedding of Tiny Tim in 1967. *(courtesy of Phyllis Diller )***

as established as Diller. She emerged from the curtain in an elaborately gold-trimmed, metallic-frilled dress that seemed to spring from *Alice in Wonderland.*

"They finally let me do [stand-up] because I feel comfortable doing that," Diller says of her last appearance. "I felt I didn't always click with him. I didn't want to risk it. Some people, for instance Charles Nelson Reilly, I mean . . . I have been positively on the floor. I don't know whether it was the problem of whoever briefed me for him or what. There were times we were sensational, but then there were times it didn't work."

Regardless of her on-camera relationship with the master host, Diller was in attendance for the ratings coup of Tiny Tim's wedding on *The Tonight Show.* Moreover, while the tapings originated from the Big Apple, she was beckoned to guest-host twice—not a happy experience either time, she recalls.

"The first time, a group of my agents came screaming into the dressing room *while they were calling me onstage!*" she says in her familiar shrill. "They had had cocktails, darling. In those days, I was young and nervous. It was a lot of responsibility. When I have to *rush* onstage after scraping off three drunk agents, I'm not in any condition to do a show. Unfortunately, they had chosen guests whom I didn't even know! Isn't that swell?"

Diller says she never misses *The Tonight Show.* During the 1960s, when she began her own television series, *The Tonight Show* was the perfect exposure of her talents.

"Everybody knows *The Tonight Show* is your major springboard to 'celebrity' or being known," she says. "From then on, it's up to you." Although her admiration for Carson supersedes criticism, she doesn't mind offering some.

"As he's gotten older, you'll notice he's extremely partial to male guests," she says with a wry laugh. Popping the punch line, she says, "Unless they are young girls that he had screwed . . . and that's where my appearances started thinning out."

# Carl Reiner

In the days of live television, Carl Reiner was busy writing comedy, performing on Sid Caesar's show, and starting his collection of Emmy Awards. Eleven in total, they presently "sit quietly at home oxidizing." His association with NBC late night began during these years with appearances in New York with Steve Allen. Then on to Jack Paar, whom he calls "an open nerve," and proceeding on to Johnny Carson. As "Mr. Guest," as he refers to himself, he liked his regular late-night manifestations, and his improvisational skills shone on all *Tonight* shows—and most prominently on *Your Show of Shows*—but he cites many differences between the two more popular late-night hosts, Paar and Carson.

"Everything Paar said had a vitality to it," he says, "because you didn't know if he was gonna explode or fall apart or anything. He was very vulnerable. Johnny was very closed."

Reiner always liked the personae, physical image, and talents of Johnny Carson. Casting what became *The Dick Van Dyke Show* in 1961, Reiner, the creator and producer, reduced the list of candidates to star in the series down to two men: Carson and Van Dyke. Carson regularly turned down such offers for sitcoms, and soon Reiner witnessed Van Dyke in the Broadway hit *Bye Bye Birdie,* concluding he would be right for the role of Robert Petrie. (Coincidentally, Carson and Van Dyke were also up for the same role in *Bye Bye Birdie*, but Carson chose not to leave the security of his *Who Do You Trust?* television series.)

The Carson-Reiner relationship remained one of friends, and since then, Reiner has appeared on Carson's show regularly. A Carl Reiner appearance with Johnny might include just about anything. Once he came onstage with a spe-

Carl Reiner wanted to make certain his appearance would be considered for the next anniversary show, so he took out scissors and proceeded to cut up Johnny's new black suit on December 12, 1979. Carson, stunned from the spontaneous stunt, did not change, and resumed the ninety-minute show with his suit in shreds. *(Wide World Photo)*

cial present for Johnny: a tuna sandwich. Another time the topic of discussion was Reiner's handsome toupee, which was removed during the show, to sample other hairpieces he had brought to seek audience approval. In the last several years, upon introduction, Reiner would burst from the curtain, perform a wild, eccentric dance that only lacked foam around his mouth, and within thirty seconds he'd slouch, out of breath, to the seat. His were not always "pluggers" for a movie or his books, because he was often hailed to appear in a pinch—which spotlighted Reiner's ad-lib talents that much more. But through the years, he's been a mainstay with the show, and he's clocked in about fifty times with Johnny, averaging little over once a year.

Reiner met Carson during the *Who Do You Trust?* years, and sometimes the Carsons and the Reiners all went out to dinner in New York; always wonderful memories, he says. "We've considered ourselves friends even though we don't see each other a lot anymore," says Reiner, "except during poker games. [Johnny] doesn't go out a lot." About the poker games between the funnymen, of whom Reiner won't divulge a roster, he does insist that Carson's a good player, and maintains "he doesn't cheat. You'd think he might because he's a magician. He probably could if he wanted to."

Professionally speaking—a slant on Carson conversation he'd rather abide—he predicted that young Carson would go far. "I knew he was good the first time I saw him," says Reiner, whose talent for perceiving, writing, and performing comedy is concrete. "He had a boyish charm about him. He always surprised you that he was so smart as he was. He looked like just a cute guy.

"Nobody knew that *anybody* could stay on television for thirty years," he says. "How did he do that?"

## Jimmy Stewart

Expectations of James Stewart have always been high; from his directors, from his coworkers, and mostly from his fans. And he always delivers. On *The Tonight Show,* no one is ever disappointed when Ed McMahon reads his name as the first guest of the night. Over the decades, he's made countless appearances, but in the last ten years Stewart has favored America with a new talent: poetry.

Wonderfully embraced by America, Jimmy Stewart the poet hesitatingly grasped

A female pretzel baker was on *The Tonight Show* demonstrating to the host the precise method of looping the strands of dough into the common pretzel shape. Carson attempted to twist the dough, but it didn't work. The lady gave him another strip of dough, saying, "Here, try this piece. I don't think yours is long enough." The audience roared at the possible implication, which of course was not intended. He quipped, "Yes, I think I've heard that before."

the crumpled piece of paper the poem was scribbled on. Out of another pocket, he pulled his black-rimmed glasses and confidently placed them on his head, where they sat starkly next to his silver hair.

One of the best poems, and certainly the funniest, was about a hotel in Junín de los Andes, a small area in western Argentina where the Stewarts were vacationing. The top step in the hotel was slightly offset, and everyone in the Stewart group who reached the top tripped and stumbled to the floor. So aggravated by the step, Stewart took to the pen to release his funny frustration, and wrote a gem called "The Top Step in the Hotel Junín (Is Mean)."

The May 3, 1983, *Tonight Show* audiences roared as he stammered through his delivery that night premiering the poem on national television.

Other poems followed: "I'm a Movie Camera," about the little hand-held he purchased for his daughters just prior to a family safari in Kenya. The camera was snatched by the jowls of a hyena and mangled around the midnight hour. In the first person, speaking for the camera, Jimmy wrote another creative narrative that grabbed the audience like the hyena chompers around the camera—by force. It was *that* good.

One of the most touching of the poems was about the dog he loved named Beau. This was a feisty golden retriever, Stewart says. "Beau was a fine-looking young pup, but we soon found out we had a problem. Beau was on the wild side. He tried to bite holes in furniture." Eventually, Beau became closer to Stewart and his wife, Gloria. He even crept up in bed to slumber between them, while Jimmy patted his head. Years later, while filming a movie out of town, Stewart was summoned and told his dog was serious-

Johnny gets word from nearby producer Fred de Cordova as he and one of his favorite guests, Jimmy Stewart, wait for the cue that the commercial break has ended. *(Globe Photos)*

ly ill; the actor rushed home. Beau had to be put to sleep. "I could hardly see to drive home because of the tears in my eyes," Stewart remembers. Suffering the loss, he thought a poem might be the best therapy to get through the pain. The universal rhyme brings to memory the favorite pet that everyone has loved.

One evening, Stewart had a cold, and his tolerance seemed low. Even his stammering seemed stuck in low gear. Slowly relating a story to Johnny Carson about a tedious eight-hour, flat-tire-ridden journey to Lake Beringo in the western part of Kenya, Stewart even tested the patience of the host. He dabbled a bit with a poem about the experience and finally gave the audience a brief treat:

> *Lake Beringo is a body of water*
> *Its surface is smooth as glass*
> *But getting to Lake Beringo*
> *Is a genuine pain in the ass.*

After *The Tonight Show* staff was hounded by letters requesting copies of each poem, Stewart was contacted by a publisher and signed a contract to assemble them in a small but mighty book. Besides, his personal office could hardly handle the requests for poems, either. Published in 1989, Jimmy Stewart and His Poems was released with a bang by Crown Publishers, Inc., in hardcover. It sold over 230,000 copies and remained on the best-seller list for weeks. Stewart toured the country, signing copies for trailing lines around bookstores and malls across America. In Chicago, he signed more than a thousand copies in two hours.

"It's the first time I've gotten into this publishing thing," Stewart confides. "But for a book like this, my publisher says it did very well."

The poem's success story began with *The Tonight Show,* Stewart explains, although it's not mentioned in the book. "I enjoy doing *The Tonight Show,* and being with Johnny so much. He's a wonderful friend. When I'd go on it, I'd throw these poems in as a sort of surprise for Johnny for the fun of it."

Inevitably, Stewart is questioned when his next book is due. He says: "I have sort of an established answer to that. I just say, for these four poems I have in this book, it took me twenty years to write these. Number one, I don't have twenty years left; and number two, they are all about special things that happened to me. It's been sort of quiet lately. So I think this'll be my final attempt at writing poems."

In 1990, near Christmas, Johnny Carson brought Jimmy Stewart on the show to finally talk about *It's a Wonderful Life,* the movie classic most associated with Stewart, his gentle charm, and the value of life.

*By Stephen Cox*

## Jimmy Stewart and His Poems

> *There's nights I watch the Carson show,*
> *And nights I'd wished I'd missed*
> *But if Johnny says Jimmy Stewart's on*
> *I watch simply because of this.*

*Of all the legendary people seen,*
*You'll recall this one as gray-haired, tall, and lean*
*He stammers and stutters, so gently with charm*
*It's his charisma, I say, that rings an alarm.*

*He has squeezed an accordion,*
*Chatted with Johnny,*
*Talked about Capra,*
*And President Ronnie.*

*But of all his talents*
*I think I admire,*
*It's his telling of poems*
*When I'm about to retire.*

*So I sit up and ready myself*
*For a tear or a bellow*
*These are* his *poems, ya know,*
*As brilliant as Longfellow.*

*He pulls out his glasses*
*And the paper scribbled on*
*He begins to ramble Stewart-like,*
*and so on, and so forth, and on. . . .*

*The words reach and touch you*
*Like the man America holds dear*
*One story tells of Beau,*
*His dog he loved in yesteryear.*

*Now, if you want my opinion—*
*Otherwise you wouldn't be reading this book*
*I suspect he's got one more in him,*
*So I browse* TV Guide *and look . . .*
*To see if aka George Bailey*
*Is on with Johnny tonight,*
*'Cause if it says, Guest: Jimmy Stewart*
*Carson's once again my night-light.*

# Betty White

She's played Jane to Johnny's Tarzan. She portrayed the first lady reporter allowed in a men's locker room. She was Eve when Johnny was Adam.

"I always accuse him that whenever Johnny wants to take his clothes off, he calls me," Betty White laughs.

One classic skit that White remembers vividly was a spoof of heavy rains in southern California in the 1970s.

"We were having terrible storms along the beach here," White says, prefacing the routine. "There was a romantic love story, a dinner for two at a beach-side café with a strolling violinist. The waves became a bit high, and they began to splash through the window a little bit."

Then more than 550 gallons of water pounded down on both White and Carson while they sat on the stage pretending to eat dinner.

"We couldn't rehearse that kind of thing," White recalls. "Fred de Cordova said, 'Now when the water hits you, pretend to fall off your chair.' When the water came down, it washed me clear across the room! Johnny thought I was dead."

Although she may not be most remembered for her stints as a Mighty Carson Art Player in more than a dozen sketches with Carson, this golden girl goes way back with *Tonight*'s host. The two chummed when Johnny was hosting *Carson's Cellar*, in the 1950s, "when he was about four years old," she says. Her memories of the earlier days are hazy, but one evening is sharply in focus.

"Johnny and I had dinner one night at Trader Vic's right before he started the *The Tonight Show*," White remembers. "Jack Paar had retired, but they had signed Johnny and had a few weeks of different hosts during the summer before he actually took over.

"Johnny was sitting there grousing, 'I wish they'd stop auditioning people for my job!'" Thirty years later, it's apparent they didn't find a replacement for the slot he hadn't filled yet.

White and Carson remained friends while both careers exploded in different directions. As White predicted, this perfectly calm comic named Johnny Carson took hold of America with the show he grasped, and the rest is history. White went on to do theater, live television, game-show appearances, *The Mary Tyler Moore Show*, two versions of *The Betty White Show*, and more recently, *Golden Girls* on NBC.

Publicizing the senior-citizen sitcom during the first season, White subbed one night for Johnny during a week of various guest hosts. "I never really did a monologue," she recalls. "There's really no one who can follow Johnny in that department. But I had an awful lot of fun on the show."

As with many actors, White wishes she could be on his final show, to bid him farewell, but mostly to thank him.

"I think the world will be watching," she says quietly. "There's been some high-rated lasts, but this one may break the book. I think it's going to be very tough and an emotional time for Johnny."

## Jonathan Winters

*A guy once said to me, "Wow, appearances on Carson are incredible exposure." So one day I took that exposure and went over to Bullock's here in the Valley and picked out an Italian sweater for $585.*

*And the woman said, "Mr. Winters? It is Mr. Winters, isn't it?"*

*No, it's Spanky McFarland, dear, and the Little Gang has turned into racists.*

*"Is this gonna be cash or charge?"*

*And I held out the palm of my hand, which was empty. She said, "I don't understand."*

*I said, "That's exposure." I told her it was forty to fifty thousand dollars' worth of exposure.*

The jovial Jonathan Winters has one observation, when quizzed about Johnny Carson: "Wealthy. Very wealthy."

And for Winters, although he's appeared with Johnny "mehnnnnee, many, many times," he admits it's not a fantastic-paying job. "Whatever I made on *The Tonight Show,* I still have on me."

Winters actually began on *The Tonight Show* when Steve Allen was at the helm and the ship was docked in New York. He graduated to Paar, and then to countless appearances over the years with his favorite host, Johnny Carson. He doesn't keep track of how many.

"Over all other hosts, I prefer Johnny," he says in a rare moment of seriousness. "I've always had a lot of fun with Johnny. Any time I'd go on, I'd come in a uniform or some crazy thing. We'd set up questions like 'What was it like when you were a kid? What did you do in school?' . . . and we'd just go from there. We'd improvise. You can't do that with everybody. I don't think I could do it with Leno, to tell you the truth."

It was only a matter of seconds when the seriousness ran dry and one of the Prince of Improv's personalities took over. "Letterman," he says, "he looks like he's been running down the hall marking all the lockers at the University of Indiana and sayin', 'Watch me Saturday, 'cause I'm gonna be at the Big Eye Club.' That's all I get from him. There's a guy that's Mr. Rudeness. He talks to Paul and throws cards through papier-mâché windows. That's his act. I'm still sayin' 'What the frig does he do?' Jesus, I don't get the man. You stand him up at Eddie Polino's in a little gig outside of Moline, Illinois—you know, for Joliet prisoners, and this son of a bitch will be torn to pieces.

"I don't deal in jokes. I deal with reality."

Some might wonder what reality Winter deals in—but not well. His humor is thrown at audiences with abandon, and it's rapid-fire, packed with plenty of punch. To appreciate Winters, one must listen closely, as with Robin Williams. When both Winters and Robin Williams appeared on *The Tonight Show* in 1991, Carson warned, "Tonight we have two deeply disturbed gentlemen on the show . . ."

Winters might show up in a Confederate Army costume or a general's uniform, armed for anything. When the curtain parts, Carson and the audience never know what sort of outlandish character resembling Jonathan Winters will emerge.

"I've come out in different wardrobes. A look is important," Winters explains, lapsing into a brief serious mode again. "We're talking about a visual medium. Obviously, today people are coming out in sweatshirts and workout suits, and Bermuda shorts and sneakers, cowboy boots, and God knows what. To come out in something so you can play off it is good."

The serious talk stops, and Winters turns "on" without hesitation with this spontaneous bit.

"I could come out as a cowboy and I'd say:

*"I wish I had time to change. I just came from the set. The last thing I did was a shoot-out. I can't even remember who it was with. God, it was fun. I jumped off a building. I remember it was the Flowers Hotel or something and jumped on to the horse and killed it. Terrible thing. 'Course, I'm a pretty heavy guy. I shouldn'tve jumped four stories, and when I hit the horse it just drove him into the ground. It was a Shetland pony. Poor thing couldn't get up. It was sad. God knows I didn't mean to do it. They shoulda had a fake horse. But apparently when they panned down, it was a fake and when they pulled it away, it was on rollers. So it looks bad in the film. I hope they don't use it."*

Winters adds: "And, of course, in the audience they're sayin', 'Did he really do this?'"

## Charles Nelson Reilly

When I called him, he immediately asked: "Did you ever see the movie *The Great One*, with Jose Ferrer? Well, it was about the demise of this great comedian. Jose Ferrer went around trying to get some nice remarks from people, and he had a terrible time."

Reilly has earned the title of the perfect guest on the talk-show circuit—or at least the most flamboyant. He's done them all, including some fifty to sixty appearances with Johnny Carson. But when he jumped over to Joan Rivers's show—opposite Carson—he fell out of grace, he says.

"Joan asked me to be on her New Year's Eve show, and I knew full well that I'd never be on Carson again," says the irascible actor. "But I directed Joan in a student thing probably in 1963 or 1964. And when she had her first television show at WOR, which was with one camera and she had black hair about twenty-eight years ago, I was her first guest ever. I have a friendship and allegiance there."

Carson "never really liked" his vaults from one talk show to another, Reilly explains. "And they would tell me that every time I went [to NBC]. Shirley Wood would say, 'Johnny's very upset that you do Merv.'"

Producer Fred de Cordova humorously describes Charles Nelson Reilly in his book *Johnny Came Lately* like this: "Charles Nelson Reilly can't be reached by phone. You have to leave a letter under his doormat; he'll call back as soon as he looks under the mat. He's often out of town for a month or so, which means that your messages may turn out to be a bit dated."

Reilly responds: "The problem I have with de Cordova is that when I was in good graces, he told me he was writing this book. He said that I was born to be in talk shows and I was fabulous. Then, when I fell out of grace, I saw the book in Chicago while I was directing an opera there. I picked it up, and he said I was impossible to reach. No one could ever find me when they wanted me on the show. All of that's not true. Of course I've got a phone.

"I was never *scheduled* on that show. Any time I was on, they would call me between ten A.M. and four in the afternoon. 'Can you get right over here?' People would cancel, or be ill, or not be able to get a plane. I was on the show so much because I'm up the street. I could get there in eleven minutes. Sometimes they'd call and I'd cancel things to go on. I was very good to them. That was my little niche there."

For years Reilly would appear sporting a fitted suit or even a tuxedo. He killed audiences with elaborate stories about adventures onstage or in Hollywood, and his delicate effervescence created a wonderful storytelling atmosphere that could be classified only

**Frenetic and sardonic, Charles Nelson Reilly usually placed himself in various catastrophes and unusual situations that nearly always convulsed the audience into screams of laughter. *(Globe Photos)***

as his own. Writer Glenn Esterly, in *TV Guide*, recalled one appearance: "Reilly portrays himself as the bewildered victim of various catastrophes, finally confessing: 'I don't know why I even came here to tell you this.' The audience laughs. Good-naturedly, Carson discloses: 'I'm not sure either,' which builds on Reilly's laugh."

"It was difficult," Reilly says of *The Tonight Show.* "You realized it was the best and you *had* to be good or you wouldn't be back. With Merv Griffin, Mike Douglas, Jim Nabors, John Davidson, Dinah Shore . . . there was no 'Johnny-ism' about it. That's why it is the best show, I guess."

Despite a talent coordinator's warning minutes before entrance ("We want six minutes of hilarity"), Reilly always turned a slow show into a racing pace of laughs, even if he had temporary caps in his mouth that day. Carson laughed right along with the audience. Reilly's quick to point out: "A critic for the *Chicago Sun-Times* did a story. He was very lovely. He listed the guests, the history of the show, and said by far I was the best guest because I made them laugh every time and laugh aloud. He said a perfect night would be Carnac, a baboon from the San Diego Zoo, Angie Dickinson, and me."

Reilly alludes to Carson's warnings to people not to appear on *Arsenio.* "That's very narrow and stupid," he says of the mandate. "Because I don't make any money in this business. I never work in things that pay money. I make my living from these game shows and talk shows. I don't go on to plug movies or TV shows. I don't make movies. I'm not on a sitcom. I just went there to help them out all the time. Joan Rivers was my friend longer than he was. What goes on between them has nothing to do with me."

"He's always been overly protective of his show . . . and I guess that's why it's the best. But he could just relax a little. He'd have some wonderful final shows if they'd look over that list they have."

## Stan Kann

Stan Kann might be one of the few individuals—like Joan Embery—who began as a "civilian" guest and became a celebrity mostly because of the *The Tonight Show*.

You might recall Kann as the collector of crazy contraptions who frantically demonstrated the objects of wonder to Johnny, and many guest hosts along his frequent tour of *The Tonight Show* decades. Kann, a former St. Louisan, was suggested to producers of *The Tonight Show* by Phyllis Diller, who also hailed from Missouri. A talent coordinator said, "Show me," and Kann flew to New York for his first appearance with Johnny in 1968.

Kann's hobby for many years was collecting vintage vacuum cleaners and strange household devices. This passion began when he was a youngster and became fascinated with his neighbor's old Ohio vacuum cleaner, which became extinct in the home around 1930. Soon, he became so enthralled with the machines, he would visit neighborhood homes and ask the housewives' permission to listen to their vacuum cleaners. He could surmise the make, model, condition, and whether the bag was full simply by listening to the whirr.

Kann thought he'd bring on his *Tonight Show* debut about twelve or thirteen different makes and kinds of vacuum cleaners. Some of the more unusual ones, which can

Crazy-contraption collector
Stan Kann frantically
demonstrates an unusual
orange-peeler to guest-host
David Brenner. *(courtesy
of Stan Kann)*

only be unearthed at antique stores, were boxed up for shipment to NBC Studios in preparation for the show.

At the studio, Kann became "terribly nervous and upset" when he realized some of the shipment arrived with half of the vacuums, and the other box was missing. He sliced right through his tie opening the available box, and demonstrated to producers a model that had to be operated manually: "You had to run with it to get it started," Kann describes the vacuum. "People in the offices peeked out to see what the whizzing motor was."

He was set to appear with Johnny in a few short hours. With only parts of the vacuums, they would wing it. Making the wrong turn in the building, and walking down the emergency exit rather than taking the elevators, Kann ended up in the underground tunnel and eventually across the street from Rockefeller Center, completely lost and nervous, sweating, trying to find his way back into NBC Studios. People were passing him everywhere.

He made his way backstage again through the audience entrance, "and the makeup man could hardly put makeup on me I was so nervous," Kann remembers.

Johnny introduced Kann first; he demonstrated an old "pump" vacuum, which the stagehands had assembled "because of union rules," he points out. Of course, it wouldn't pick up any dirt. "Then I threw down angel hair on the floor. It wouldn't pick that up, either. I tried to step over to get another vacuum and my pant cuff got caught on another vacuum and it tripped me and I fell. The audience went wild. "I was mortified," Kann says. Orchestra leader Skitch Henderson was falling off the piano seat, laughing.

Next, Kann demonstrated the Regina "bubble machine" that you push and run with, activating the motor. "It made a *chugga-chugga* sound when you pushed it," Kann says.

While in St. Louis for a stage show appearance in March 1967, Carson was cajoled into attending a party at the home of frequent *Tonight Show* guest Stan Kann (center). Noticeably, Carson becomes withdrawn at parties and large gatherings. It was during this party that a Missouri hypnotist was photographed speaking with Carson and later the photo was utilized in brochures advertising the services of the hypnotist. Eventually, Carson sued for removal of his image from the advertising matter and won the case. *(courtesy of Stan Kann)*

"When I gave it a shove, the handle fell off, and it went past the desk, off the platform, and across the studio. The audience was in hysterics."

Kann's first of what went on to total seventy-seven appearances lasted over sixteen minutes. Other talk shows flew him in to demonstrate wacky gizmos on their programs. Mike Douglas. Merv Griffin. Dinah Shore. He did 'em all, he says.

Audiences loved the character of Stan Kann almost as much as the devices he displayed. He rattled around like Don Knotts in a haunted house, sweating, tripping, and stammering his speech. His voice quivers and shakes, and then rises a few pitches. Sometimes he's yelling over the audience's maniacal laughter. "It *is* a character," Kann agreed. "Because they never wanted to give you enough time. You had to go like a bat outta hell on those shows. Especially *The Tonight Show*." While frantically showing guest-host Bill Cosby a cheap kitchen contraption that sliced pineapples, he broke the prop and quipped, "Well, I like canned pineapple. . . . Nothing wrong with that!"

At home, he's quiet, witty, calm, and figidety. His domain in Hollywood, where he moved in 1976, is a penthouse suite atop one of the 1920s apartment buildings, next to the complex Mae West once owned and resided in until her death. Antique radios, vacuum cleaners, and vintage paraphernalia adorn the room, but tastefully, if that can be imagined. He and his cat, with one paw declawed (a result of a mix-up at the veterinarian's office), live comfortably, he says.

Recalling his Tonight Show appearances, Kann says he prefers Carson over all of the other hosts he's appeared with. He's dropped in on Joan Rivers, Joey Bishop, Bill Cosby, David Brenner, and one night he'll never forget, when Don Rickles was the host.

One of the items displayed that evening was a little battery-operated toy train that ran around on a track on any surface, floor or desk. "I wanted to show you could even use it without the track," Kann says. "I put it on the floor, and the camera followed it. Rickles said, 'All right, Stan. Enough of the train, Stan! Let's do something else, Stan! Ya got some more toys, Stan?'

"I went to grab the train, and the cars came loose from the engine, and it kept going," Kann laughs. "I went to go for the engine again, and it got away from me."

Rickles, tactful man that he is, ran over to the little train and smashed it to pieces with one foot. He picked up the wreckage and said, "There, Stan. Take it and fix it. You'll have much more fun trying to put this damned thing together."

Not openly mad, Kann admits he's never found another train like it. "I wanted to use it again," he says.

On another night when the moon was full, Kann brought on a Yoga Wheel, for those who wanted to practice the exercise and meditate, but not turn themselves upside down and balance in the position. David Brenner was the guest host and Kann convinced Brenner to strap himself into the large metal contraption. "It turns up and stands you on your head, and locks you in different positions," Kann says, describing the machine.

As the last segment of the show, Kann attempted to jiggle the brake and release the host, but the brake was locked. Stagehands tried to pry the metal unhinged, but nothing worked. "We had to bring a mike over to him and have him say good night—and tape a preview of the next day's show—while we tried to release him. He signed off that way."

Guest-host Joey Bishop watches Stan Kann nervously demonstrate one of his crazy props. *(courtesy of Stan Kann)*

# The Joan Rivers Feud

The many faces of Joan Rivers (circa 1965). *(from the author's collection)*

**❝** *The way Johnny found out about my new talk show was horrendous. I wanted to be the one to break the news to him. . . .***❞**
—Joan Rivers
*People*, May 26, 1986

**❝** *I just felt she could have handled it differently, that's all.***❞**
—Johnny Carson
*Los Angeles Times*, July 6, 1986

To recap an event that swept the press into an exciting duel of sides and words between celebrities and Hollywood power brokers, the Joan Rivers/Johnny Carson feud began when Rivers suddenly announced at a press conference that she would be launching a late-night talk show in September 1986. The new program would start at 10:00 P.M., giving it a half-hour jump on *The Tonight Show*, and backers at the Fox Broadcasting Corporation boasted that Rivers would tap an audience that's ripe for picking: younger viewers.

"But what 'youth-oriented' has to do with Ms. Rivers is anybody's guess," wrote reporter Bob Wisehart. "She doesn't have the vaguest idea how to attract the viewers she needs to succeed."

So what if Rivers decided to compete with Carson? Many other talk-show hosts did. Joey Bishop did, and returned to guest-host for Johnny on *Tonight*. The opportunity has been given to many, and failed by all. Television's morgue is littered with the bodies of those who attempted to bump the King: Dick Cavett, Mike Douglas, Les Crane, Alan Thicke, Pat Sajak, Merv Griffin. The only close contender has been Arsenio Hall in recent years.

The bottom line indicated that Carson was angry that Rivers was negotiating to renew her contract with the Carson company at the same time she was cutting her own deal with Fox. Carson was upset by "how she handled the announcement." When she let America in on her new endeavor, she let her mentor in at the same time. As executive producer Fred de Cordova put it, "A secondhand discovery that a member of your family has moved out of your home doesn't make for joy and celebration . . . . Her manner of saying bye-bye to Johnny and *The Tonight Show* was, in my opinion, somewhere between tacky and tasteless." Staff and cohorts on the *The Tonight Show* set were shocked and surprised.

To clearly comprehend the impact that this falling-out had on both Rivers and Carson, one must go back to 1965, when Rivers was a thirty-one-year-old "groveling outcast," as she describes herself, "struggling through mud up to my waist to break into show business, going through humiliations nobody should have to endure".

Rivers's life changed on February 17, 1965, when she was slated to appear as a guest on *The Tonight Show*. She had been writing for Allen Funt on TV's *Candid Camera*, toying with nightclub gigs, writing material, and attempting to hit it big. When *The Tonight Show* finally gave her that long-awaited chance with Johnny, she was excited and nervous, and moreover, unconfident. She described her initial thoughts in her book *Enter Talking*, which she dedicated to Johnny Carson for "making it all happen." Rivers recalls:

*I did not allow myself any emotion. I had been through the excitement before, been through the rush of adrenaline and the dreams, and knew the predictable end. Twice before I had been in the very same studio for Paar and twice I had been a failure.*

That night, Carson wiped his eyes from the tearing of laughter, and told her, "God, you're funny. You're gonna be a star." Rivers says the words did not register at all. She only heard them later when she watched the show with her parents. Her thoughts did not include a fantasy that this would be the beginning process of her adoption into the *Tonight Show* family. But that's exactly what was brewing.

Rivers says that night was "the moment when my life began, when seven years of rejection and humiliation paid off, when I got past all the people who were saying I was too old and would never make it." Her destiny had been prescribed by Dr. Carson, NBC.

As Rivers describes her relationship with Johnny from then on, it was a "curious" one. They saw each other rarely on social terms. In front of the camera, they clicked. During commercial breaks when the camera's red light went off, they had nothing in common. Carson would sit silently drumming his pencil on the desk, and she'd say, "Gee, doesn't the band sound great tonight?"

"And yet the relationship has been deeply precious to me," she said in 1986. One of her fondest memories of Johnny Carson, she told *TV Guide* reporter Mary Murphy, happened off the air: "In appreciation for an appearance he made on her pilot in 1968, Rivers sent Carson a gift—her baby daughter, Melissa Rosenberg, wrapped in a white blanket. Melissa was carried into Carson's office at NBC accompanied by a note that said: 'I weigh 4 lbs. 3 ounces. I eat very little. Please bring me up Jewish.' Carson took the baby in his arms. Immediately she fell asleep and Carson was afraid to wake her. For two hours he held her in his arms. 'How's that for a sweet guy?' Rivers asked."

Through the years, her appearances were steady; good shots. Her style differed greatly from Carson's, which was the reason he enjoyed her on the show. Her comedy, her monologues, were popular with audiences, and a younger crowd did start to emerge from the stable that Johnny had built. Her wit was seldom without sting. ("Elizabeth Taylor was so fat they had to grease her thighs to shove her through the Golden Arches at McDonald's" . . . "God didn't mean Jewish people to exercise and bend over, or He'd have put diamonds on the floor.")

"Sure she's strident," Carson told *Los Angeles Times* writer Paul Rosenfield. "What she does is in total contrast to what I do. I am not going to ask Joan Collins her age. Joan can get away with that. It makes sense for her. But seven or eight weeks a year is one thing. It would be difficult for Joan to do this full-time, and she knows it. She admits this—she's said herself that her style would become too obvious if exposed every single night, 52 weeks a year."

Carson was right, and ultimately Rivers was correct also. When she decided to curtail her position as *The Tonight Show's* first permanent guest host—employment that began in August 1983—she was commandeering terrific ratings, terrific salaries, and exposure to beat 'em all. She also knew she would be taking a chance. So did Fox Broadcasting.

Rivers professed to be loyal, and she "swore" she'd never go up against Johnny. Things at NBC and Carson Productions in 1985 were not all well, she says, a year before her announcement; Johnny's contract was solid for two years, hers was only for one. "That shook me to the very

Joan Rivers is the guest host of the Halloween *Tonight Show* in 1985, with Pee-Wee Herman as Count Dracula, Phyllis Diller dressed as Dr. Ruth Westheimer, and Elvira in the hot seat. *(Personality Photos, Inc.)*

roots of my confidence," she wrote in a special reply to the feud printed in *People* magazine. "It could only mean one thing—the powers were uncertain about my future." Moreover, Rivers held in her hand an NBC interoffice memo that listed possible successors to Johnny in case he did not renew his contract. Her name was not on it.

She thought she should seek new employment, with a steadier nature, and in essence began hedging her career to counterbalance the employment, so as to limit any risks. But after all, she was in show business. Nothing's steady. Everything's a risk.

When Fox Broadcasting approached her about hosting her own show opposite Carson, she decided to consider the offer for her own survival. She accepted, and much later rejected the NBC offer, which was submitted late in the process.

In his autobiography, *Johnny Came Lately*, Fred de Cordova described the events surrounding Rivers's drop of the bomb:

*Monday, May 5, 1986, Joan (and Edgar on extension) called me at home at 7:00 P.M. Tearfully, she had "something to tell me": she had made a deal with Fox to do a talk show. It would start in October. It* would be on the air opposite Johnny. She was calling me first and would shortly call and tell Johnny and Peter Lassally, in that order. I was stunned. All I could say to Joan was, 'You're kidding!' She told me how dear I was to her—Edgar said the deal was for three years and there would 'always be a candle in the window' for me. I repeated, 'You're kidding!' Then I called Johnny immediately. He had just received a call from NBC boss Brandon Tartikoff telling him that Joan had, indeed, made a deal with Fox and a press conference was scheduled by her for the next day. While John and I were talking, he was told that Joan was on the other phone. He said he wouldn't take the call—it was "a little late in arriving . . . about three months late."

Since that phone call, and another when she did reach Johnny—but he hung up after she addressed him—she has not spoken with him at all.

Eventually, *The Late Show* did not score the ratings Fox had hoped, and Rivers's three-year contract was shortened while lawyers settled with Rivers for the remainder. The show's demise consisted of a few more hosts and a few retitlings before a few roses in mourning for the late-night rival to NBC. Rivers's life took another sharp turn when her husband of more than twenty years committed suicide and her career began to fall apart.

In the early 1990s, with a new face assisted by plastic surgeons, Rivers has picked herself up, tucked herself in, honed a "gossipy" repertoire of jokes and style, and succeeded in a syndicated daytime talk show that produced for her an Emmy Award for excellence.

Talking to *Donahue* audiences in 1991, Rivers commented on the five-year-old Johnny Carson "feud." After her husband's death, she said, she was amazed that she had not heard "a syllable from Johnny Carson. Never."

Rivers added, "I put all this behind me. I had met Edgar through Johnny Carson. And no matter what had gone down between us, I think at certain points in people's lives, you pick up a pen and say this is terrible. . . .

"When Johnny's son died so tragically, I picked up a piece of paper and I wrote to him and said, 'How terrible, how sad, these events happen in our lives.'

"No, I never heard a word," she responds to the host's question. "It was disgusting, and it was wrong, and it was his problem."

Joan Rivers briefly hosted her own talk show for the fledgling Fox Broadcasting network, rivaling her mentor, Johnny Carson. Here, she converses with actor Stacy Keach on October 22, 1986. *(Photo by Eric Heinila; courtesy of FBC)*

# 4

................................................................

# Civilians

❝ *The monologue is very important . . . comedy material is very important. [John-ny's] favorite kind of guest is the elderly lady, the very amusing—not necessarily precocious—child. Somebody who is not just a performer in the arts. It's a piece of gold to him.* ❞

—Fred de Cordova
Executive Producer, *The Tonight Show Starring Johnny Carson*

It's been said, but most often observed, that Johnny's at his best when he's interviewing the frail and feisty old ladies, the elderly—and sometimes sarcastic gentleman, or the little kid that's invented food tape because her "brother's burritos kept falling apart."

They all keep Carson on his mental toes in an interview and deliver a challenge to him. He meets the challenge, ad-libs with the best of them, and what the audience witnesses are some of the most charming moments in television since Art Linkletter's line "Kids say the darndest things!" on the 1950s daytime variety show *House Party*.

Around the offices of *The Tonight Show,* these guests are known as "civilians." There's no military connection at all, it's just a friendly term to mean "nonperformers." There is a staff of two to three who scour newspapers subscribed to from across the country, and basically keep an open-door policy to suggestions of candidates. *The Phoenix Gazette* may have the perfect story about the eighty-three-year-old man who collects cowbells. Or *USA Today* may have run a piece about a woman who runs a nut museum. Then someone comes in the office with a newspaper clipping from somewhere in California about a fellow, John Twomey, who plays songs with his hands, cupping them, squeezing air that sounds like normal bodily functions into tunes like "Stars and Stripes Forever." "Great guest!" the talent bookers agree. "How do we get 'em?"

The variety of civilians and their peculiar talents is astounding. And usually the skills or collections they hold *are* of an odd nature. Just when Johnny assumes he's seen it all, he's asked every question, he's delivered every retort . . . someone from Middle America surprises him. Rarely have civilians made two appearances, but themes have been featured throughout the years. Annual civilian stops include the winners of the National Yelling Contest, children inventors, and cowboy poets who narrate their stories for ever-attentive audiences.

One of the more elaborately planned civilian spots was the appearance of a man named Specca, who spent nearly six hours in Studio One setting up seven thousand dominoes in a design that encompassed nearly the whole backstage area behind the

Spiderman Danny Goodwin of Chicago made headlines in 1981 when he successfully scaled the 110-story Sears Tower and was arrested for the daring stunt. *(Personality Photos, Inc.)*

colored curtain. The dominoes were individually laid in rows by Specca; they spelled out Johnny's full name, as seen by a camera above.

That evening, the band played a bit softer, and everyone walked on tiptoe backstage while the domino king watched over his creation during Johnny's monologue. One shifted domino or California tremor could stop the whole flow, or worse, scatter the single-file pieces and ruin the effect.

Finally, the moment came, and Carson was hesitant to "ruin" the setup by flicking the first domino. "I almost hate to do this," he said. When he triggered the motion, the clicking of tripping dominoes was heard through the studio as the camera followed the stream. It lasted for two and a half minutes while the intricate intersections rambled on. One section included an amazing eight rows of dominoes interweaving and falling simultaneously. The audience silently watched while holding its breath, it seemed. When the last domino fell, the audience applauded the young man, and Carson was amazed.

Another evening, in April 1979, kept the audience in silence, however, not out of amazement at a stunt, but from a fiery mishap. Karate expert Richie Barathy was on the show to illustrate how he could smash blocks. He had just smashed thirteen granite blocks that were set afire with burning oil when his sleeve attracted some of the flame. Carson and others around the stage rushed to help smother the fire on his clothing. But Barathy suffered second- and third-degree burns.

*Johnny sits among the residents of Essex, Arizona, a tiny town in California near the Arizona border, known to be one of America's last outposts without TV service. Because television could not get to Essex due to mountains that bar the TV signals, NBC brought almost the entire town of sixty-one residents to attend a taping in 1977. (Wide World Photo)*

The coordinators for the noncelebrities have vast resources, rooting out just the right civilians to meet face-to-face with Johnny and regale him with tales. Some guests have "frozen" when they met Mr. Carson for the first time in the hot seat with cameras on, red lights flickering, and an audience in mild expectation of something funny. More often than not, the civilians steal the attention and run with it, leaving even the most popular actor who is guesting that night sinking in the cracks of the couch.

Carson's secret at the game here is his ability to become a chameleon and adjust to each guest. Johnny is informed ahead of time by the talent coordinator

what each guest is like, all based on a pre-interview: Are they talkative, funny, loud, obnoxious, or serious? Or maybe they clue him in to what will set off the guest into a hilarious tirade. This rattles around in his mind briefly before meeting the civilian on the air. The guest is usually excited about the appearance and has been flown in for the all-expenses-paid trip to Los Angeles, which includes limousine escorting.

Johnny is keen to surmise just the proper approach with each guest. Rarely is his aim off. With kids, Johnny slumps in his chair, leans close to them intimately, like a pal ready to "play." His guard is down, so theirs falls, too. And rarely does he criticize *any* guest, which creates a comfortable aura from the start.

With the elderly, he has the ability to scan them immediately, assess their mood, figure their age and level of sarcasm, and then zoom! The interview, in no time at all, is lively, funny, and once again Carson's knack to draw out the best in every guest shines through. Up until 1981, his oldest guest was 103-year-old Tillie Abrahamson of Van Nuys, California, who told him; "I'm three years younger than the telephone." A few years later, Mildred Holt, age 105, appeared on the show. Carson has a theory about the civilians, he told *Rolling Stone* in 1979: "I like to work with elderly people and children. I don't know why," he told reporter Timothy White. "Maybe it's the vulnerability of them. There's a charm about older people that sometimes is child-like, and I enjoy them because, first of all, they can say anything they want to, which is just great. Age gives you a leg up on what you can say, because you don't have to account to anybody. You've lived your life and earned the right to sound off. They'll say, 'Oh, well screw that, I don't like that, that's a lot of shit.' And they lay it right out."

Carson has never come out and pinned one or two as his favorite civilians in the thirty years he's hosted the show. He's assisted the selection of a handful for each anniversary show, but those may be for pure laughs' sake and comedy effect rather than personal preference. Fred de Cordova, on TV's *Later* with Bob Costas, revealed his two favorites: an elderly lady who played the piano and wouldn't stop long enough for him to

Johnny assists 105-year-old
Mildred Holt onto the stage.
*(Globe Photos)*

jump into a commercial; and Frank Hill, from South Carolina, who specialized in making jewelry out of quail droppings. Dressed in huntin' cap, untucked plaid shirt, and jeans, Hill, who spoke with a thick southern drawl, presented a large star-shaped pendant to Johnny and told him, "I'm a gonna break da mold . . . that's a first limited edition. It's a *biiiiig* droppin' for a *biiiiig* star," he proudly told Johnny.

"I don't think I've ever been so moved, if you'll excuse the expression," Carson said, examining the gift. "You're kind of the Cartier of caca, aren't you?"

The group known as civilians who have appeared on Johnny Carson's show is an elite class of individuals, indeed. There have been hundreds of them, in every age group, and from every state in the Union. Here are a few you may remember. The first civilian hails from Barrow, Alaska, way up north where the Eskimos roam.

- **Fran Tate**, owner of Pepe's North of the Border, the only Mexican restaurant in Barrow, Alaska, ap-

Louise Gaddis, eighty-eight, and Elsie Stahly, eighty-seven, the remaining students of Danvers High School class of 1918 in Danvers, Illinois, pay a visit to Johnny in 1988. *(Personality Photos, Inc.)*

peared with Johnny on March 24, 1984. She was booked on the show based on an article that appeared in *The Wall Street Journal* about the hassles and trials she encountered attempting to open a fast-food restaurant in the northern tip of Alaska, where the population is three thousand and it's twenty-four-hour darkness from November through January. McDonald's turned her down.

Tate is feisty, funny, and she even brought Johnny a few Eskimo artifacts to examine.

Alaskan Fran Tate shows Johnny a walrus usig. "Let's just say every male walrus has one," she told him in March 1984. *(courtesy of Fran Tate)*

One item, a walrus "usig," is the male sexual organ on the walrus, which is highly collected up there, she says. Tate presented the object, which resembled a bone, to a suddenly stymied Carson, who blurted, "Some place, there's one *unhappy* walrus!"

Tate spoke of the success of her independent eatery, the pros and cons of living in northern Alaska, the twenty-foot-high snowdrifts and all. Her appearance lasted extra long, because it was going so well, she says.

Following her, actress Amy Irving was the guest. Carson reminded Irving that he heard she bathed nude in the French Riviera on a special, private platform. "What were you doing there?" he asked the actress.

"I was waiting for some walrus with a million dollars," she quipped.

- One evening, the guest was potato-chip collector **Myrtle Young**, who brought along some of the character-shaped munchies she's preserved while working in a potato-chip factory. She had one that was shaped like a dog, another was a sleeping bird with its head nestled to its breast ("cute"), and she even had a chip of Yogi Bear. Of course, Johnny noticed Yogi's head had been glued. "Yes, I broke his neck," Young said.

Young looked—and even laughed—a lot like Edith Bunker from *All in the Family*. (Wouldn't this be the perfect plot for an episode of the show, anyway— "Edith Goes on *The Tonight Show*"?) Young displayed her tray of fragile chips and gently held them up for the camera for all to see. When Ed McMahon diverted her attention, Johnny reached for a chip from a bowl, chomped on it like a proud Pringles commercial actor, and scared his guest into a frenzy; Johnny held up the

Four-year-old spelling champion Rohan Varavadekar of Houston, Texas, captured the host's heart in 1987. Johnny asked Rohan his favorite words, and he responded by spelling words such as "inextinguishable," "abbreviate," and "biochemistry." Rohan, who correctly memorized Johnny's own birthday, was planning to celebrate his fifth birthday the next day. He asked Johnny if he could come to his party, being held at Disneyland. *(Wide World Photo)*

fresh bowl of chips. Laughing almost uncontrollably at the prank, Carson almost couldn't swallow the chip he'd popped into his mouth. The audience was in hysterics.

- Johnny introduced four-year-old spelling champion **Rohan Varavadekar**, of Houston, Texas. The bespectacled little boy, dressed in a bright blue warm-up suit, was there as a kid—no three-piece suit for this guy. He was all boy, uninhibited, puckish, well mannered around the adults. This captured Johnny's heart, especially when it became obvious the little chap had done his homework on Johnny.

"... When, when I read a book about you and when you were thirteen, you used to do magic tricks," he said to Johnny. "Can you show me some?"

Carson reached into a pocket for a coin, made it vanish in his hands, and then pulled the quarter out of little Rohan's left ear. It was like an uncle and a nephew on a Sunday afternoon family reunion; the audience cheered right along. Johnny even offered to show him how the magic was done, after the show.

"How do you really make it disappear?" the boy asked.

Johnny answered: "You get married."

- In February 1988, a spry ninety-eight-year-old gentleman named **Merrit Heaton** from Illinois stepped out from the curtain and chatted with Johnny about the old days and how the times have changed. The subject of women and fashion came up. Heaton, who resembled Floyd the barber on *The Andy Griffith Show*, said, "My gosh, when I was young, we'd be tickled to see a girl's ankle!"

Johnny asked him about his family. "How old's your son?"

"Oh, he's seventy-eight."

- **Minnie Black**, from Kentucky, was invited on the show to tell Johnny about her collection of gourds. Johnny noticed she brought along her own special something to quench her thirst on the show; he inquired innocently about the contents.

"I had to bring a little somethin' along to help me with my congestion," she said with not a hint of hoarseness. "You want see what that is?"

Johnny smelled the the tip of the coffee mug and puckered his whole face, looking at the band. The audience roared with laughter.

"This is booze!" he said. "Do you brew that yourself in Kentucky?"

"Now listen . . . Kentucky is known for their good bourbon . . . but I take that for medical purposes."

"How often do you get that congestion?" Johnny quipped.

- **Barney Odum**, from South Carolina, brought his pet "Flatnose," a large bulldog, on the show to display the canine's talent. Ol' Flatnose was supposed to be able to climb a tree 15–20 feet high, which had Doc Severinsen in disbelief. Severinsen told Carson before the show, "If he climbs this tree, I'll kiss his ass."

  For the stunt, the prop personnel stabilized a large, bare, twenty-foot tree in the middle of the stage, and connected a stuffed animal at the top for Flatnose to retrieve when he reached its height. Odum cajoled his dog, "Get up there, Flatnose, get up there. . . ." And sure enough, this feisty bulldog scaled the tree like a rising elevator; Flatnose was clinging to the tree bark with all his might. When the dog reached the top, the audience cheered.

  Then the audience began to laugh as Doc sauntered over to the middle of the stage with a grin on his face.

  "Doc, I'd like you to meet Flatnose," Johnny said.

- In 1985, self-appointed International Queen of the Polka **Vlosta Kersik** sent Johnny a color snapshot of herself playing the accordion atop a cow in the middle of the pasture. "Now this is my kind of guest," Carson laughed, holding up the photo for the camera.

  Kersik had written polkas for Pope John Paul II and Ronald Reagan, she said. She wanted her chance to serenade Johnny on the show, so she was invited; talent coordinators probably hadn't planned on such a hilarious segment when they made her travel arrangements.

  Kersik, an outspoken, witty, buxom redheaded woman, appeared on the show in a homemade, wildly colorful exotic dress. She had an accent, possibly Polish, and told Johnny how she tests her new tunes on her husband. "I wait when my husband takes a bath," she says boldly. "Then I'll take my accordion, sit on the toilet seat, Johnny. . . . Honest! Honest!" By that time, the audience, and Carson, were laughing so hard, the rest of her sentence was not audible. Later, she took center stage with her electronic accordion and sang her ditty, "Johnny, Johnny, Come an' Dance wit' Me . . ." which was really a pretty catchy tune. It had Johnny bouncing.

- The rather large, tall female police officer named **Cathy Crumbley,** who was running for sheriff in Belmont County, Ohio, came out and greeted Johnny and Ed one night donning a cowboy hat, holster, and boots. At first glance, she was not one to mess with, but her voice and manner were as gentle as . . . a rookie's.

  Crumbley started to sit down, but decided to remove her holster before she did. While standing, she had some trouble with the buckle, so Johnny came around the desk to assist her. He helped unfasten the buckle, and innocently quipped, "This is

- Johnny Carson returned from a commercial and said, "As I mentioned earlier, this lady performed one of the most famous classic roles in movie history. She was Walt Disney's Snow White. . . . Will you welcome **Adriana Caselotti.**"

  Caselotti, trim and young-looking in her seventies, was as animated as her most famous role. It was the occasion of Disney's sixth reissue of the classic animated film to theaters, and Caselotti was happy to appear with Carson.

  During the interview, Johnny made the mistake of asking Caselotti if she ever found *her* real Prince Charming. Not one to lie, Caselotti told her tale of dating a foot doctor, Dana Costigen, when she was very young. She left Costigen, married another man, and divorced. Then she married Norville Mitchell, remained married for twenty years, "and he died unfortunately." Then she called the foot doctor, married him soon after, "then he died."

  "You don't think that after hearing this on national television, anybody else is gonna marry you, do you?" Johnny asked. "That's like saying, 'Good-bye, Charlie!'"

  It was all in fun, says Caselotti, who did not mind the Carson quip, or the studio audience's raucous laughter. Later, she sang a line of Snow White's operatic singing and segued into an impromptu version of "Oh Johnny," which the band joined in with melody.

  "Is that what killed the last two husbands?" Johnny asked.

  Still, she didn't mind another crack about her late husbands, because she was just as comedic about it. "He apologized on the show, and I said, 'No, it's perfectly all right,'" says Caselotti. "He was so nice."

- **Bertie McKay**, 103 years-old, stepped out slowly from the curtain and automatically lifted her elbow so as to give Johnny the signal that she needed assistance. Incredibly agile at her age, she walked past Johnny's desk and made a beeline to kiss Ed McMahon and compliment him as host of television's *Star Search*. She gawked over Big Ed. "I look at ya every Sunday," McKay professed to Ed, nearly ignoring Johnny. "Every Sunday. Oh, I love your program." Of course, Johnny acted sullen, while the audience laughed.

  Into the interview, Johnny said, "You have a sister, I'm told."

  "Yes," Bertie replied, "she's dead. I'm sure she's dead. I had her cremated."

- On the eve of Valentine's Day in 1991, Johnny had **CF Corzine**, from Centralia, Illinois, on to talk about his unusual habit each February. Corzine, age seventy-seven, and resembling a thin Santa Claus (and he's played the jovial Christmas hero for many years, he says), was brought to the attention of the Carson producers by St. Louis television reporter John Pertzborn.

  For forty years, Corzine has sent the exact same twenty-five-cent Valentine card to his wife, retrieving it and resending it annually. Naturally, Johnny asked the obvious: Why?

  "I wanted to get my money's worth," Corzine shot back.

  He brought along the simple card, which has no special meaning attached, he says. It had been canceled and tattered by the post office so much, the address wasn't readable. Corzine admitted his wife has been so sick of the card, she attempted to throw it away a few times; so he hides it after he presents it to her each year.

Possibly the funniest part of the show, however, involved his name. When Johnny guessed what CF represented, Corzine explained that CF stood for nothing. When CF had attempted as a teenager to enlist in the army, the officers said they *had* to put something on paper, so it was officially registered: "C-only F-only." For years, he was called "Cone-ly Fone-ly," and receives mail thus addressed even today.

The show went extremely well, and ran overtime, bumping another scheduled guest. "Being on the show didn't make me nervous until after it was over with," Corzine says. "After we got back to our hotel suite, Mr. Carson had sent to me an enormous bouquet of roses, and the card said, 'For a gold performance.' Wasn't that sweet?"

- St. Louis barber **Bill Black** was scheduled to show Johnny items from his unusual hobby—objects made from human hair—however, time ran out, and Black became one of the "bumped" in 1991. He stayed over to appear the next night, when Jay Leno was mysteriously and suddenly called in to guest-host.

CF Corzine, of Illinois, the man with just initials for a first name, sent the same valentine card to his wife for forty years. He explained his habit to Johnny on February 13, 1991. *(courtesy of CF Corzine)*

"I was told there had been some death threats to Carson," Black says. "They had special agents and a lot of security backstage, I noticed. I took a picture of my name on my dressing-room door, and Security came running over to me when they saw the flash. They wanted to take my camera away."

Black showed Leno his items instead, although he was disappointed in not meeting Johnny. Black wore his necktie made of human hair, the tassels on his shoes were hair, and he brought a vest that could be worn. Black even wears a hairpiece.

"You don't make underwear, do you?" Leno asked.

- Quadruplets **Allison**, **Brooke**, **Claire**, and **Darcy Hansen**—all sixteen years old—streamed out from behind the curtain and sat on the couch one night in 1991 to talk with Johnny. The beautiful girls, all very similar in appearance and donning flowery sundresses of matching material, were flown in from San Antonio, Texas. After the expected Do-you-fool-your-friends? questions, the payoff came.

St. Louisan Bill Black creates objects from hair, such as the hairball he shows Jay Leno. "It's the psycho barber, ladies and gentlemen," quipped Leno. *(courtesy of Bill Black)*

"Somebody told me you have sort of a strange relationship with *The Tonight Show*," Johnny said.

Answering in unison, they finally deferred to one sister. "We understand that we were conceived while our parents were watching *The Tonight Show*," she said, as the audience laughed. She added, "During the monologue."

"That bad, huh?" Johnny said. "Did your parents remember anything about the show?"

Another sister answered, "Tommy Newsom was leading the orchestra that night."

"Yeah, Tom has that problem," Johnny said. "When he's on, people often leave and go into another room."

- "I think this is the first time we've had a toilet trespasser on the show," Johnny said, introducing **Denise Welles** to the show in 1991.

Welles had attended a George Strait concert at a Texas arena when she noticed the women's rest room had a thirty-foot-long line at the entrance; Wells couldn't wait and entered the nearly vacant men's room. "So I just went in," she says. "There were probably six or eight gentlemen in there."

"What was their reaction when you walked in?" Carson asked.

"They all had their backs to me. . . . I don't know," she snapped.

*The Tonight Show* audience was screaming.

A police officer in the men's room caught her and reminded her of the city ordinance forbidding any entrance "in a manner to cause a disturbance." She was arrested. Her plea was necessity, she claimed. "I wasn't window-shopping."

"I think the correct term is *comparison* shopping," Johnny said.

Welles's turmoil did not stop at the arena. After she was kicked out of the concert, her picture and an accompanying story were run on the front page of the *Houston Post*. Morning radio shows poked fun at the story on the air. At work the next day, she says, her cohorts put a sign on the men's room: MEN AND DENISE ONLY.

# Johnny's Mug

One night, Johnny was visibly upset. His coffee mug was missing. Usually, it sits right there next to the two-headed pencils he taps, and the wooden cigarette box, by the lighter and the microphone. His desk set is rarely disturbed, but this night his coffee mug was distinctly absent.

Someone asked him where they come from. He shook his head and said, "I don't know."

"We have our name on the bottom," says Alma Olney, owner of the Burbank Mug Shop. "He's not very observant."

When her husband, Robert, died, Olney assumed the mug-making business he had begun in 1972. It still operates from the same building, converted from an old lawn-mower shop in Burbank. Still young at seventy-one, Olney runs her business with excitement and a sense of adventure. Her most famous product, although it's rarely advertised, is the mug that bears the face of Johnny Carson . . . seen nightly by millions of viewers.

In 1974, Jack Grant, the propmaster for *The Tonight Show*, wandered into the shop and asked if a picture could be applied to a mug. The Johnny mug was thus designed, and the same shop has kept their most famous customer in tan-and-brown ironstone beverage containers ever since. Until 1991, the photograph was a 1970s close-up of Carson leering to one side. Recently, he changed it to a current photograph. It's possibly the most famous coffee mug ever made, although for most watching Johnny Carson, Java is the last beverage they crave before sleep. Nice mug. Wrong hour.

"Johnny's mug is the worst," says Olney of its actual construction. "Just a horrible thing to work with because of the concave surface." She pulled out a little paper decal reminiscent of the water-soaked tattoos children used to buy in bubble-gum packs. The decal is soaked in warm water, applied to the mug with a small squeegee, and finally fired in a kiln for permanence.

She estimates there might have been five hundred mugs produced since 1974. The mugs regularly disappear from the set. They are given away. Johnny has autographed a few for charity auctions, and a few have been broken along the way. Remember when Dolly Parton knocked one off? How, you ask? Don't ask. On countless occasions, animals have jolted the mugs from the desk with their hind legs.

These little treasured mementos of *The Tonight Show* are not easily obtained. NBC does not market them—or any *Tonight Show* memorabilia—in the gift shops next to *Late Night* sweatshirts or *Cheers* beer mugs. No Johnny Carson T-shirts or posters are found. His mug has remained a sacred item that is produced exclusively for Carson Productions, although Olney admits that a few have "disappeared" over the years.

She has designed and produced mugs for other shows: *Goodnight, Beantown, Our House, Falcon Crest, Matlock, Sweethearts*. Her clients also include large corporations such as Lockheed Aeronautical and MCA Corporation. She has over five thousand mugs in her shop from which to choose.

Pictures on her shelves attest to the celebrities who have commissioned her work: Sammy Davis, Jr., Don Rickles, Carson. Each portrait is signed, although Carson's to her husband was forged most likely by a secretary ("For Bob—Best Wishes, Johnny Carson.") Olney still hangs the portrait with pride, because her husband was such a fan.

In the eighteen years her company has produced the mug for Carson, she and her husband attempted to reach the star twice. Both times they met with no success.

"My husband served as the mayor of Burbank in 1981 to '82, and he attempted to contact Johnny Carson by telephone," Alma says. "He just wanted to say hello as mayor, introduce himself, and also remind Johnny that he made his mugs. He could never get through.

"Years later I wrote him after my husband passed away, but he never responded. He never acknowledged that Robert Olney made his coffee mugs. Robert was a big fan, though. We teased him once, when he was working in the back; we told him Johnny had just walked into the store. He went out there all excited, and no one was there."

Olney continues filling orders for Johnny's mug. The last order was for several dozen—the largest order yet. She applies the name decals on the guest mugs, which read GUEST 1 and GUEST 2. Ed McMahon's has ED on the reverse, and Johnny stares at his name in Gothic type each night as well. Jay Leno had a special request on his: no picture, just the word "Manimal."

Hundreds of letters per year are marked "Mug Request" and delivered from NBC to her shop. She has sold a few in the past to persistent fans, but Carson Productions has warned her not to mass-market the item. "I'm not making a living on Johnny's mug, that's for sure," she says. "People write from all over for these, and it's been delivered to me for years. What do they expect me to do with it?" Alma has saved the boxes with letters from across the country. She's even become friendly with a few writers and corresponds regularly with them.

G. P. Wiser of Yelm, Washington, recently wrote with a mission for the mug: "If they had been astute enough to forward my letter to you, this letter would not be necessary. . . ."

Another woman from Williams City, North Carolina, wanted to know whose picture is on the mug and how much a mug would cost. From Sulphur Springs, Texas, a woman asked if she could exchange a Raggedy Ann doll she handcrafts for a mug. Alma traded.

# 5

..................................................

# Carson's Wild Kingdom

**" When he has an animal on, he hopes it craps. "**                    —Tony Randall

It's a wonder none of the animals that Johnny ever held up for the camera leaped from his grasp and went for his jugular. Naturally, he's been nipped on the hands a few times by rodents and squirrelly creatures the proper names of which no one can pronounce, let alone remember. But blood has never been drawn during an appearance of Joan Embery, the San Diego Zoo's animal ambassador.

"I've never had anyone injured on *The Tonight Show*," Embery says of her nearly eighty appearances with Johnny Carson. "There have been other animal people on the show, and I've heard stories about accidents . . . but not with me." Every imaginable critter has appeared on his show: from aardvark to zebra with everything in between—except, perhaps, a panda.

Embery says it is Carson's nature and professionalism that ward off attack by beasts visiting the show. (He may exercise this magical control on more than just animals.) He never prepares for the animals, refusing even to pet them before airtime. Still, he maintains control of otherwise unpredictable situations with the animals, though to viewers, his composure seems almost effortless.

"It may not look like Johnny is in control, but he is," says Embery. "He's a master at what he does. All you have to do is work with everybody else in the business to know and appreciate that."

During the transfer of animals from her arms to Johnny's, Embery keeps close watch as the animal moves. If she instinctively feels the animal is restless and the situation is "dicey," she says, she may proceed to the next animal abruptly, a transition the audience rarely notices. And Carson trusts Embery completely. He has to.

It's during the handoffs backstage that the trickiest part of the creature's *Tonight Show* debut occurs. One lion cub couldn't handle the band behind the curtain, so his appearance was nixed. A monkey ran amok backstage once, so that chimp lost its chance. But mostly the animals are carefully selected for their meeting with the keeper of the late-night kingdom.

"Johnny's a very willing participant, but he also has the sense to know when to back off and give them a little space," says Embery. Many hosts she's worked with throw themselves at the rare creatures she introduces before they have time to settle; as a result, the animals become defensive and sometimes hostile. "I've never really had that feeling with Johnny."

The animal segments are some of Johnny's most popular with the viewers, who sometimes wish it were they holding the baby monkeys. *(courtesy of Joan Embery)*

**Joan Embery, *Tonight Show's* animal ambassador.**

Embery points out that Joan Rivers has, on occasion, ridiculed or degraded animals, attempting to be funny. "The audience takes that to a point, but when you go overboard with it, the audience rises to the defense of the animal, and it backfires on the host or the comedian," she says. "Some hosts, on *The Tonight Show* or on other shows, just don't know that line."

Viewers imagine themselves cuddling the little baby orangutans that Johnny loves so much, wishing they were in his shoes. But many might not realize the restraint he practices for the camera. In the case of the hairy tarantula that crawled up Johnny's arm, both Embery and the host held their breath.

"I find them fascinating creatures, but I don't like handling them," Embery says. Craig Tennis, the talent coordinator who first brought Embery to the show, recalled the spidery incident.

"Of all the animals Joan eventually brought, the one that undoubtedly caused the most revulsion and fear—even in Joan—was the tarantula," he says. "Now, one of the things that Johnny always does best is to appear terrified and shocked by animals, which, in fact, he is not at all. In this case, I think he was somewhat repulsed."

Embery gingerly picked it up and put it on Johnny's hand as she squirmed inside but attempted to keep her cool for the camera. Embery told Carson it would not bite unless alerted or maddened by something, and even then it would be like a wasp sting—but still painful. It moved around, then climbed at a quick pace up to his bare neck beneath the television lights as the audience at home held its collective breath.

"Exactly what kind of thing might I do that would annoy it?" Carson quipped on cue.

A butterfly collector was a guest on the show one night. The fellow showed some frames to Johnny that displayed the colorful butterflies under glass. Johnny asked, "How do you mount a butterfly? It must be very difficult."

The real star of the November 4, 1971, *Tonight Show* was Carol, the four-year-old Asian elephant that Embery escorted to the studio with the help of two assistants; Carol rode in a horse trailer for three hours, amid mad Los Angeles traffic, to get there. Craig Tennis had heard about the peculiar talents of this elephant from a story that ran on the Associated Press wire service. The elephant was trained to paint with a brush, creating a mural of colors on the floor.

*The Tonight Show* that evening was taping in Burbank on a trip West; New York was still home. Tennis noted that Carson enjoyed the elephant's appearance, "because he learned very early on that if he put a handful of peanuts in his pants pockets, the elephant would smell them and keep going for Johnny's crotch with his trunk."

Johnny is amazed at Carol the elephant's ability to paint. *(courtesy of Joan Embery and the Zoological Society of San Diego)*

Carol was one of Embery's favorite animals ever. She had helped raise it, and the young elephant was her buddy. "Interestingly," Embery laughs, "in the first few years, people used to call me Carol, and I'd say, 'No, Carol is the elephant.'"

The night before Carol's performance, Embery was worried that the studio audience might frighten the elephant. Carol had appeared in public before, but not quite in this atmosphere. Would she react adversely? Would she be petrified? And all the talent coordinators and producers kept wondering was, "Would she paint?"

Embery recalls: "I started getting really jittery the day before the show, and I was up all night getting my clothes ready and studying the notes I'd made on each animal. I've spent the night before almost every *Tonight Show* that same way. I'm especially nervous if there's little time to prepare, but even if I have everything ready, I lie awake for hours, thinking about what I'm going to say."

**Joan Embery introduces "Boom Orang" to Johnny on her first appearance.** *(courtesy of Joan Embery and the Zoological Society of San Diego)*

She was also thinking of the time, just four months prior, when she rode Carol's back in a Fourth of July parade; the five-foot elephant, weighing in at a ton and a half, took off at a trot and nearly plunged into the side of a house.

Backstage, the pachyderm's giant ears were perked. Although clearly nervous from the mirrors that surrounded her onstage, Carol, soothed by Embery, held brush in trunk and painted with enthusiasm on cue. The audience loved her. She splattered colors on the floor everywhere, including over Johnny's shoes.

Also on the show that evening were a baby orangutan named Ken and a hairy-nosed wombat. A wombat looks like a rodent, "but it is a marsupial, a member of that group of mammals, including the kangaroo and opossum, that raise their young in abdominal pouches," Embery explains.

Ken, the innocent, baby-faced orangutan, nicknamed Boom Orang, was a hit. Carson loved cuddling this bowlegged little baby with big, expressive eyes.

Another guest on the show that evening was Dudley Duplex, a two-headed California king snake that was about eighteen inches long with black bands running crosswise around his body. Indeed, this snake had two functional heads, the result of an "incomplete twinning process," Embery explained on the show. She handed Johnny the snake, and he lost his grip. It started to crawl up his sleeve. It was with this animal, Embery explains in her book *My Wild World* that she first experienced the expertise of Johnny Carson:

> *Johnny widened his eyes and rolled them back; then his expression froze and he went rigid all over. I thought of the keeper in the reptile house who had warned me, when I arranged to take Dudley to the show, that he was quite rare and I had to make sure nothing happened to him; in my mind's eye, I*

*could see the keeper watching the show. What if, in his fright, Johnny some-how hurt the snake? Immediately, I reached over to grab Dudley, but very subtly, Johnny put his hand on mine to stop me, and I realized that he'd let the snake crawl up his sleeve. I sat back and watched with some astonish-ment—that moment probably marks the beginning of my appreciation of Carson's professional genius—and when Johnny had had his fun, he stood up and shook his arm and the snake slid out. It turned out to be an incredible spot—one that people remember to this day.*

The funniest bits with animals are those that are spontaneous—which, by far, is most of them. "When you force something or try to make something happen with animals, it never works," Embery believes. The key booking for one evening was a koala bear—cute, furry, and funny. The audience cooed over the bear. But the real screams came when the next guest, a little marmoset tropical American monkey, crawled from Johnny's arms atop his head and stayed there. Embery had just finished commenting that they love to climb. It was perfect timing, as the cameraman secured a close-up of Carson sitting still with this little monkey perched on his head. As Embery removed the little marmoset, it started to dig at Johnny's scalp and hang on to his hair. There was more. Johnny felt something funny and patted his hair. It had dribbled; it had marked its territory with its scent on Johnny's head. The audience was in hysterics, while Johnny's deadpan "Why me?" face stared right into the camera.

Birds of a feather have mostly flocked together when appearing with Johnny Carson. A few have actually sung, like the big green parrot that warbled "I Left My Heart in San Francisco," or the parakeet that was trained to do impressions of a cat and dog, by meaning and barking. Then it called out, "Here, kitty, kitty, kitty!" Those were rarities. Most of the birds have been uncooperative with Carson, who always saves the situation with a joke, which is usually at least as funny as a perfect feathered perfor-mance would have been. After witnessing a silent bird one evening, he joked in his next mono-logue:

"We had a nice lady on last night from British Columbia with her pet parakeet—supposed to speak a hundred and fifty

**Joan Embery and a visiting koala bear. *(courtesy of Joan Embery)***

**With a California condor in 1984.** *(courtesy of Joan Embery and the Zoological Society of San Diego)*

words. The bird didn't do nothin'. After the show, it was too bad, I finally got the bird to talk . . . just as I was sealing him up in a Shake 'N Bake bag."

One night, a scheduled guest had flown in to Burbank for an appearance with his pet parakeet. The guest had invited a companion to accompany him to California. At the Sheraton Universal, where the guest, the companion, and the bird all stayed the night, the bird freed itself from its cage and flew over near the pillow of the owner's companion. The fellow rolled over, flattening the little bird, and it wasn't discovered until the morning. Nonetheless, Carson had the guest on the show to explain, and as a gift, Carson had purchased a beautiful new parakeet for him to train, with an invitation to return. Recapping the situation a year later, the guest appeared again—this time more cautiously, and without a companion in his hotel room. The bird spoke up, but still the funniest element was retelling of the first pet's accidental demise.

Transporting the guest nonhumans can sometimes lead to problems, like the time Joan Embery and seven guys loaded a giant Galápagos tortoise into the back of a van for the three-hour trip to NBC studios. The giant turtle began crawling over the driver's seat on the highway, Embery says: "It wasn't fast, but it was very powerful, so we had to stop him, pull over each time and move him."

Jim Fowler, usually clad in African safari garb, has also appeared numerous times to feature an exotic animal that he has procured from a private collection or "borrowed" from an animal institution in the United States. Usually, his are more of the exotic-type selections like large bats. Fowler has appeared on behalf of Mutual of Omaha's "Wild Kingdom" program and does not work for the San Diego Zoo.

All totaled, a flurry of hundreds of animals have popped into the *Tonight Show*'s living room to settle in Johnny Carson's arms or relieve themselves on his desk. Naturally, the latter prompts Carson's perfect ogle of embarrassment into the camera, which is funnier than anything the animal could ad-lib. Johnny has welcomed pygmy hippos (which excrete a slimy substance that becomes quite messy during appearances), rhinos, a hundred-foot snake, and even opossums. Carson's favorite? The apes.

Once, Embery strolled out two five-month-old baby orangutans in a twin baby carriage. They were fitted in diapers, with little bows affixed in their hair, and they couldn't have been sweeter. Johnny embraced them in his arms and hugged them. One orangutan kissed him in return and wrapped its long arms around Johnny's neck and hugged him back. Then, as Johnny laughed at the baby orang's innocent expression, it delivered a perfect comedic stare at Johnny, à la Jack Benny, which made the audience erupt.

Another appearance featured a sloppy kinkajou (akin to an organ-grinder monkey) that climbed on top of Johnny's shoulder and chewed a banana, leaving a mess on Johnny's maroon sports coat. Then the little guy, the kinkajou, that is, climbed up on Ed's head and ate a banana. Ed was apparently thrilled that one of the animals, outside of an Alpo pup, finally noticed him sitting on the couch.

Milking a baby hippo, Johnny tries not to get his suit wet. *(courtesy of Joan Embery and the Zoological Society of San Diego)*

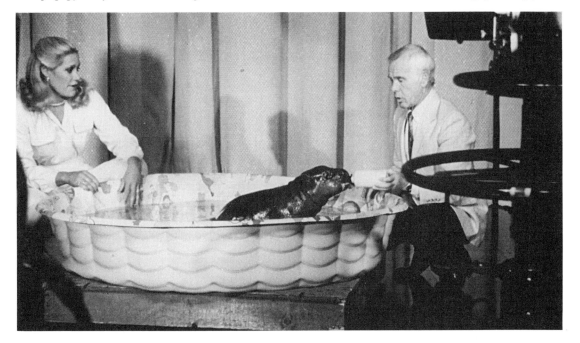

> It was Beauty and the Beast one evening when Johnny had five Miss America
> contestants, among other guests, on the show. After the monologue, he said: " .
> . . and on our show tonight we have five Miss America contestants, and also
> some dogs [audience roared] . . . I mean real dogs [more laughs] . . . come on
> now, you know I mean dogs that bark!"

Precautions and timing are everything in her business, Embery says of televised appearances with animals from the San Diego Zoo. "We're not talking about trained Hollywood animals here," she adds, in a serious tone. "These come from the wild, and may have been born in captivity. Some in their adult stage might not be safe to handle in a live studio situation. Timing is everything."

Luckily, she reports, no animals have escaped the grasp of her, Johnny, or the assistants, and lunged into the studio audience when she was appearing. She carefully chooses unique animals with a stringent set of criteria because *The Tonight Show* is the zoo's most popular showcase, and also extreme care must be taken for all parties involved—but mostly for the animal.

More caution was exercised by Ed McMahon and Johnny one night when an animal trainer, whom McMahon leaves unnamed, had brought a calm-looking jaguar on the show, held back only by a chain leash. "He came in quietly enough . . . but there seemed to be no way the trainer could hold him," says McMahon, who wondered if the jaguar might leap. Johnny was supposed to scoop fresh vanilla ice cream—the jaguar's favorite—from a gallon drum, put it into a bowl, and place it in front of the big cat. "At the same time, I happened to glance at the trainer and said, 'Johnny, I don't think he's hungry.' This surprised Johnny, who looked at me," McMahon recalls. "I pointed to the trainer's hand. There was blood pouring from three long, deep scratches. The cat had already clawed him."

Johnny looked at the blood and said, "Yeah, you may be right. He's probably not hungry. Anyway, it's too late for ice cream." He quickly topped the ice cream with the lid, and the jaguar was not asked to return as a guest, needless to say.

In the five-minute spots, which can run longer, knocking other guests off the show if all is going too well, Embery admits she "teases" audiences with an animal. "I can't educate the world in five minutes," she says, "but we can develop a curiosity, and then if I can get the public through the gates of the zoos, it's their job.

"I like to think what I do on *The Tonight Show*, as far as developing people's interest in wildlife, is good for all zoos," Embery says. "Johnny's done a fantastic job showing what we have, but [the San Diego Zoo] has an image to uphold, and we want people to see us in a certain light. Anytime you mix that with entertainment, that's like walking a tightrope with animals. I try to keep that balance."

An aspiring veterinarian in the 1960s, Embery, now forty-three, began her stint with the San Diego Zoo in 1968, giving lectures and traveling with animals. Later she set aside her yearning to become a vet. She enjoyed working with animals at the zoo

Feeding a baby kangaroo, Johnny was gentle with the little marsupial with powerful hind legs. *(Globe Photos)*

and has remained their "goodwill ambassador" since. Her expertise in the animal world has taken her to almost every zoo in the United States, and to many television studios as well. She has introduced animals to Steve Allen on his TV show, and to Art Linkletter, Dinah Shore, and Virginia Graham. Shows such as *Good Morning, America*, *PM Magazine*, *Hollywood Squares*, and *Truth or Consequences* have asked for her to stop by—with a little friend or two, of course. Embery even made guest appearances with animals on episodes of TV's *Alf* and *Newhart*. Surrounded by animals on her horse ranch (which includes Clydesdales, quarter horses, and miniature horses), she also has a Labrador retriever that keeps her and her husband company.

# The Matinee Lady: An Unsolved Mystery

*Carol Wayne's death is unsolved, certainly. But I don't think it was a drowning. A drowning, yes, of course, but there's more to it than that. . . .*

—William LaCoque
U.S. consular official
Manzanillo, Mexico
June 1990

One of the most popular recurring comedy sketches on *The Tonight Show* was the "Tea-Time Movie" with lecherous Art Fern, played by Carson donning a jet-black wig and wielding a stick he loudly cracked at the table. His sidekick was the "Matinee Lady," a buxom blonde beauty named Carol Wayne, the master of the double entendre with a squeaky voice that invoked a dumb-blonde characterization.

Wayne made more than a hundred appearances with Carson, and became the butt of on-air jokes about her bountiful breasts. Her eye-catching figure, smooth skin, and flashing eyes made her a perfect comic foil for Art Fern in these sketches. Writer John Austin commented, "Carol Wayne's forte was her ability to make innocent statements seem suggestive. If [Wayne] asked somebody if they would like a cup of coffee, it sounded as if she was asking them to go to bed with her."

One night on the show, Wayne announced to Carson during a sketch, "I had my first big affair . . . I had forty people." Of course, the audience went into hysterics, because her delivery was good. Another night, Wayne was talking to Carson about a beer commercial she had done when she told Johnny, "I never knew those beer people were so fussy. If your can isn't turned just the right way, they let you know." After the audience settled down, she added, "Then they have special stuff they spray on your can to make it look wet and delicious."

Offscreen, Wayne reportedly became very friendly with her boss, Carson, and speculation about their relationship lingered. In a February 1984 *Playboy* photo layout and interview, Wayne noted of her employer's divorces and her own: "There was always bad timing." she noted of her divorces and his. "He loves me,' she said. "I love him. It's an understanding, a given. He still sees me every day in his dreams. When he shuts his eyes, what does he see? Me!"

Albeit confusing, these quotes might have been part of a mystique she attempted to create between herself and Carson. One writer speculated it was her personal fantasy. Carson never publicly voiced any feelings about his sidekick of many years, although reportedly he was "quite shaken" when he was informed of her death.

When Carson cut the length of *The Tonight Show* from ninety minutes to sixty, the Art Fern "Tea-Time Movies" began to diminish, and finally halted. Wayne's appearances on NBC were limited, and she finally declared bankruptcy in Los Angeles on December 13, 1984, due to a heavy cocaine habit and an increased abuse of alcohol that hastily depleted any funds she had built up. She was divorced, lonely, and seeking work. Reportedly, around this time comedian Richard Pryor, a friend, had offered her a role in his upcoming film on the stipulation that she check into a drug and alcohol rehabilitation unit—all funded by the comedian. Then the news hit.

"The fully clothed but horribly bloated body of Carol Wayne was found floating in a sun-drenched Santiago Bay at Manzanillo on January 13, 1985," writes John Austin in his book *More of Hollywood's Unsolved Mysteries*.

Austin continues: "Fisherman Abel de Dios was casting a net from his wooden fishing boat about 300 yards out in the bay when he spotted the body floating no more than twenty feet away. When the body was brought

**Buxom blonde Carol Wayne as the "Matinee Lady" with Johnny Carson as "Art Fern," in a regular skit in the 1970s known as "Tea-Time Movies."** *(Personality Photos, Inc.)*

ashore in a police launch and identified as that of Carol Wayne by employees of the Las Hadas resort, Edward Durston, with whom she had checked in earlier in the week, could not be located. A few hours later it was discovered he had left for Los Angeles two days before Wayne's body was discovered. Strangely, he deposited her luggage at the airport, saying she would 'pick it up in the morning.'

Attempting to dry out on her own, Wayne accompanied Edward Durston, a Los Angeles used-car salesman, down to Mexico for a stay in January 1985. Near the end of the trip, on January 10, the couple were separated because of a dispute about accommodations: which hotel to stay overnight in before departing at a nearby airport. After a heated argument, Wayne headed out to the beach for a walk. Durston checked into a hotel. That was the last time anyone saw the Matinee Lady alive.

According to authorities, Carol Wayne had been dead about thirty-six to forty-eight hours when she was discovered by the fisherman, and tests proved negative for traces of drugs or alcohol in her system. The waters of the Santiago Bay where she wandered were quite gentle and shallow. Austin noted: "Wayne would have had to wade out 250 to 300 feet just to reach water four feet deep." An accidental fall was ruled out by Deputy District Attorney Arturo Leal, who said that nearby were two outcroppings of rocks on the beach, but Wayne's body showed no signs of cuts or bruises. The case remains a mystery to all parties who investigated the death.

**The death of actress Carol Wayne, a member of the Mighty Carson Art Players, remains a mystery.** *(from the author's collection)*

Writer Austin also pointed out: "It was Durston who was with another aspiring actress the night of October 4, 1969, when she either jumped or fell from a sixth-floor apartment window near the Sunset Strip." That actress was Diane Linkletter, daughter of the famed TV host and huckster, Art Linkletter. Reported as a suicide related to LSD, Linkletter's case has also remained a mystery.

In his book, reporter Austin raises suspicious elements surrounding Carol Wayne's death:

- "How could Carol Wayne, who could not swim and never liked to be near water, drown in a calm, shallow bay? This was a tragically ironic demise, especially considering the clichéd joke she inspired around *The Tonight Show*, 'With that chest, this lady will never drown!' "

- "Could Carol Wayne have had her head held under water until her lungs were full and she drowned?"

- "Why did Durston take Miss Wayne's luggage to the airport before he left, rather than leave it at the hotel awaiting her return?"

- "Why did Durston leave Manzanillo while he knew Wayne was still missing?" (No missing persons report was ever filed.)

Wayne was forty-two when she was found dead. In the late 1950s, she and her sister Nina were professional ice skaters with the Ice Capades until Carol suffered an accidental fall on a skate blade, ripping a five-inch gash in her left knee. The two eventually worked as Las Vegas showgirls at the Folies Bergère. The sisters crept into television, landing Nina a role on the sixties TV sitcom *Camp Runamuck*; Carol would later land an occasional spot on *The Tonight Show*.

Married three times, Carol had one son, Alex, with her second husband, Bary Feinstein. Her last, unsuccessful marriage was to producer Burt Sugarman, and ended in divorce in 1980. Sugarman later married *Entertainment Tonight* coanchor Mary Hart in 1989.

# 6

......................................................................................

# "Good Stuff"

*❝ The monologue truly is the pride and joy of his appearance on the show. I think it developed from the God-given ability to read a newspaper and see one day before the American public what their attitude would be the next day. ❞*　　—Fred de Cordova,
*Later* with Bob Costas

It's true, Johnny's sense of gauging the American public's opinions and mood is incredibly accurate. Maybe we're fooled. Think of it this way, is it possible he's the leader and the public are the followers? The power of the medium is wielded with the mighty hand of Carson, no doubt of that. He's been called television's most powerful man. And with good reason. He's proven the notion many times, from the toilet-paper incident that shook America's households—or bathrooms—to the paycheck he collects from the network.

The power is in the words. And most of the words come lumped at the beginning of the show in what has become a word directly associated with Johnny Carson: the monologue. Some are *his* words, other bits are the creative products of his team of writers who have handed him pages of material earlier in the day. Whatever the source, Carson molds the material into one 7-minute speech that has kept America listening and watching after TV's news for nearly 30 years. More people absorb that monologue than absorb most presidential fireside chats. They may flip the set after the golf swing, but some profess they only need their fix of Carson for the night and then it's time for sleep. All is well with the world then.

He's a magician, we know. But where do the jokes, the observations, the stories, the ad-libs, the jibes, and the newsy and sort of gossipy updates all come from? And how are they delivered so well, most of the time?

His delivery is his own. It's a mixture of Jack Benny, Bob Hope, Harry Truman, John Kennedy, Don Adams, Tom Poston, Will Rogers, a few others, and the other 50 percent is pure John Carson. His "editing and timing" he learned from Jack Benny, he says. His executive producer, Fred de Cordova, explains he "has an innate ability to see humor, sarcastic sometimes, just plain funny other times, of what the foibles of the world are. He can mold that into an observation that later becomes of serious importance."

His observation on December 19, 1973, may have been in jest, but that didn't lessen the importance when thousands of Americans flew into a panic. This was the year of the great toilet-paper shortage, if you'll remember. He was talking about shortages of a different nature. He said in the monologue, "But have you heard the latest? I'm not kidding. I saw it in the paper. There's a shortage of toilet paper."

On his twenty-second anniversary as host of *The Tonight Show*, Johnny Carson poses with a mural of many of the characters he's portrayed in sketches on the show. *(courtesy of NBC)*

"Thus began the second chapter in what may go down in history as one of the nation's most unusual crises—the toilet-paper shortage," reported Andrew H. Malcolm of *The New York Times*. "[This was] a phenomenon that saw millions of Americans strip every roll of bathroom tissue from thousands of grocery shelves."

The shortage was full of humor and fear, and it was a rumor-run-wild that caused a buying binge and a mass case of hoarding across the country. Shoppers were checking out with forty-dollar toilet-paper purchases in some cities. Carson never realized he would create such a consumer calamity when he made the remark, which was actually rooted in a "paper shortage" reported by the Government Printing Office. After news reports debunked the trailblazing rumors, the country eased its buying.

Mostly, Johnny's material comes from his writers. When he joined NBC in 1962, along with the contract came a staff, a studio, a secretary, a network to back him . . . and the writers. He thanks God for them.

Granted, Johnny Carson is naturally amusing in front of an audience. He can wing it when he needs to, and proves it when the writers' material fails. Or when he impressed audiences with his own stuff—the write stuff—during writers' strikes a few years back. And don't think the writers pen the words that dig Johnny out of the hole some nights. That's his expertise. Even on the rare nights when Carson doesn't bat a thousand, he can rescue himself with a word or a simple expression. Writer Bill Cosford noted that's his "most acclaimed skill—his ability to extract humor from all but the most desperate on-camera situations." When a joke falls flat, he not only retrieves it, he juggles it for extra laughs.

Those instances are rare, but they happen. And his unique talent for the quick save seemed to occur more often in the last five years as host than in the beginning. Some of his writers felt he did not rely on their material enough. And the blame can be put on the audiences some nights. The excitement is usually there, but not always in full force, and not always physically evident. Regardless of the show's pace, his emergence from the test-pattern striped curtain was usually greeted with long, steady, wild applause, especially after a week or two in absentia.

Usually, he'd open with a quick shot to settle the whooping crowd, like:

*Thank you . . . Look, I . . . C'mon folks [raising hand] . . . Sorry, but I was warned never to take applause from strangers. But be honest, after two hours in line, you would applaud a box of stale Wheat Thins.*

Or maybe this one after his wedding in 1972:

*Listen . . . you really must stop, because I have to have the Applause sign back in my honeymoon suite. . . . Now, Ed, I want to talk to you. I don't like to do this on coast-to-coast television, but enough is enough. We've known each other for fourteen years. I have great affection for you, but it was not necessary to stand in my room on my wedding night going "Hi-yoooooo!"*

Or this one for the nineties:

*I know . . . I know your type. You're good at foreplay, but how will you be after we consummate the monologue?*

Johnny Carson had actor Tony Randall as his guest one night. Johnny asked Tony to read a cue card for the next commercial, Camelon panty hose. Randall read: "And now here's a word about a panty hose that fits almost any man or woman. . . . " Later in the show, a bewildered Carson held up a Kodak camera sign and accidentally blurted, "Now here's a word from Kotex . . . *Kodak!*"

After a few amenities ("How are ya, folks?"), the actual printed word would kick in. Just below the camera's eye was a long wooden barrier that propped up cue cards stretched in front of Johnny. (Stenciled on the back in white was: TONIGHT SHOW JOKE-BOARD.) The cards were lined so he could jump from one joke to another, but not necessarily in any order. That's all part of his editing, you see. If the "Liz Taylor's wedding" jokes aren't working so well, proceed to another topic. With a cue-card boy, he would have to wait for the next card, interrupt if necessary, and ruin the timing of it all. These cards had sentences, sometimes just cue words, written in bold black Magic Marker. Most nights if you examined closely, you could see the keenly visioned Carson glance down at the cards to pick up the next topic. He didn't squint to read them, but sometimes when he turned to look at Ed, he'd take a quick peek.

Then the meat was introduced to America. No one but Carson and the writers knew what would be said, not even Ed McMahon—which explains his hefty, barrel-chested "ho-ho-ho." It was sort of like Santa with a few beers in him. He actually enjoys Carson's humor, like the rest of us hearing the jokes for the first time.

Even the writers never knew exactly *which* jokes were going to be used each night, explains one of Johnny's most prolific in the stable, Pat McCormick.

Their mechanics were this: The team of writers might meet during the day—but not always for a brainstorming session. Sometimes it was playtime, but the work still had to get done. McCormick explains: "We'd meet as a group. Some guys just did monologue work. I did routines *and* desk spots, and monologue. We'd pitch a consensus of stuff and write up the ones we liked. We'd get his approval on the routines first. Johnny had his own ideas, too."

For the monologue, the writers separated to their hideaways and produced. They'd write, they'd toil or scream. They would do whatever they had to do to put their share of matter on paper. This could be maybe thirty or thirty-five jokes, typed. Written, if you were really in a hurry. Faxed, if you were out of town.

Then, by 3:00 P.M., with the writer's name at the top, the jokes were handed to the Man and he gathered the papers, convened to his office, and whittled a monologue. From a team of six or eight writers working each day, he may have used eighteen or twenty of the jokes from those submitted. It always varied. The only way to find out your "score," if you were keeping track, was to watch the taping, or wait till the evening and cry—or celebrate—at home. Pat McCormick was one of the few writers who waited until the five o'clock hour to witness the monologue.

"I got into doing that, kind of a habit," McCormick says. "I'd see him just before the monologue and maybe tell him a joke or two [usually off-color]. Not everybody did that. You'd kind of figure it out," he says of the backstage etiquette around the host, just before a monologue. "I'd stand by in case he wanted to talk. But you didn't force it on him."

Describing the famous monologue, *TV Guide* reporter Bel Kaufman wrote:

> *This is often the best part of the show; it's the voice of Middle America. He comments on topical and local events, criticizing what is currently safe and popular to criticize: the postal service, British royalty, air pollution and our own Government, which he claims is his best source of humor. His political comments are irreverent without being rebellious or abrasive. They are not to be underestimated. His bite is often sharper than his barb; his barbs are pointed, but not poisonous. His accurate gauge of the country's political climate keeps him from taking risks; he avoids extreme positions.*

The monologue is always happening here, and now, because it's written the day of the show, just hours before it's aired. The Tonight Show may be the closest thing to a live show. But its news is not always relevant and current. It might be a Monday night "Best of Carson" or a string of the same on a vacated week while Johnny's in England for Wimbledon competitions. And nothing is staler than yesteryear's news.

There is competitiveness between the writers and their gems that Carson debuts, McCormick said without a hint of denial. "The competitiveness was to look at the count," he says. "I did pretty well most of the time. Like anybody else, I had streaks."

When the California earthquake—the big one—in 1971 hit and rumbled the visiting Carson crew at NBC, McCormick's opening line eventually became a classic. Johnny came out and said, "Due to today's earthquake, the 'God Is Dead' rally has been canceled."

"I did the earthquake monologue almost solely," McCormick brags. "The next day, Johnny thanked me for it."

Writer McCormick, who occasionally put on a costume or two and appeared on the air with Johnny during his ten-year stay with *Tonight*, became a specialist in the Art Fern spots. He also suggested the heavy-handed soap opera parody "Edge of Wetness," a routine that scanned the audience while Carson read utterly insulting and embarrassing narratives about the fictitious townspeople of "Sludge Falls." The soap-opera concept, which worked well for Carson, was originally a routine that McCormick had provided to Jonathan Winters for some television specials in 1964.

And "Stump the Band" usually meant Johnny threw out the routine that night. Questions from the audience written on little blue cards had the same meaning.

**During one monologue, Carson stated, "You know on New Year's Eve, most people are prone (audience laughs) . . . not that kind of prone . . . I mean susceptible to liquor!"**

One of the less frequent routines was "el Moldo," a half-wit psychic played by Carson donning a cheap black wig and a black cape. El Moldo would sit center stage, while Ed would choose random participants from the audience. El Moldo tried to guess what was on the mind of the participant, or an item Ed had chosen to be deduced. It was the Amazing Kreskin gone awry:

> ED: *El Moldo, would you guess [participant's] hometown?*
> EL MOLDO: *Yes. I'm working on it now. Concentrate . . . I see . . . Chicago.*
> ED: *No!*

Discussing a sketch back-stage in this snapshot taken in 1977. *(Personality Photos, Inc.)*

EL MOLDO: *I didn't say you live there, I said I saw it! How quick they are to jump down el Moldo's throat! El Moldo almost had it this time: "The word city is coming in very strong. . . . You are from Kansas City? [wrong] Oklahoma City? Rapid City? Sioux City? Dodge City? You once drove a Dodge through a city?*

Some of Johnny's favorite routines involved his rapid-fire delivery of tongue twisters that he had practiced only minimally but could spit out like a machine gun. The most famous, perhaps, was a parody on Dragnet with guest Jack Webb. It was called the Copper Clapper Caper, a quick exchange of tongue twisters that progressively got worse for both Carson and Webb.

As the story went, there had been a robbery at the Acme School Bell Company. Claude Cooper, a kleptomaniac, had copped Carson's clean copper clappers that were kept in the closet.

WEBB: *Who first discovered the copper clappers were copped?*
CARSON: *My cleaning woman . . . Clara Clifford.*

During a series of *News Updates* routines, Johnny portrayed a TV anchorman delivering these beauties—quickly, and without flaw:

*But first . . . is there a royal divorce in the works? Will Prince Chuck chuck Di? Will Di chuck Chuck? Or would Britains rather die and upchuck than give Chuck and Di up?*

*. . . And later we'll have film from our roving reporter, Pete Polk, who went to Pikes Peak to take a peek at Pike, then to peek at Topeka, Topeka State Park, then to Pocatella to take a poke at Pocatella then to Tacoma, Potomac, Paduca, Tumcumcari and Weasles . . .*

All of the credit for a decent monologue or routine cannot go to the writers, McCormick maintains. "Like his writers, Johnny's aware of everything that's going on," he says. "He's a very good editor. He might hand us back a routine or jokes and say, 'Not quite there yet,' and reject it temporarily. He's open to all kinds of things. He's not adverse to doing something wild."

Neither is McCormick. That's his reputation. Audiences may just know him as a former judge on *The Gong Show*, or the fellow who dressed up as Cupid, or the NBC Peacock in a few routines with Johnny. Many don't believe it, but he's a Harvard graduate. Other writers, and associates who have known him, describe him as crazy, wild, and completely unpredictable. Maybe the Robin Williams of the backstage set—only not as wired.

Former *Tonight* talent coordinator Craig Tennis says: ". . . any story you hear about Pat McCormick is probably true, provided it's too gross to tell outside of a men's room, and even then, it's probably been cleaned up. Pat is without a doubt one of the best comedy writers in the business, even if he is rather consumed with the humor of bodily functions."

A few Pat tales:

"According to legend," says Tennis, "when his baby was christened, Pat presented the nude child on a silver turkey-serving platter, all surrounded with parsley."

To a rookie writer on the show, who wished to remain nameless, McCormick prescribed a cure for pubic crabs: "You shave exactly half of your pubic hair. Then take a match and light the other side on fire. And when the crabs come running out of the fire—stab 'em."

Greg Fields, former *Tonight Show* writer, described his first meeting with Mc-

Comedy writer extraordinaire Pat McCormick occasionally put on a costume for *The Tonight Show,* or took clothing off, like the time he streaked Johnny during the monologue. Here, McCormick plays an Easter bunny, Jaws, a spring chicken, a Thanksgiving turkey, Cupid, and the NBC peacock (center). (courtesy of Pat McCormick)

> **One blooper triggered another as Johnny told viewers one night during his monologue: "You know, the queen is in town." After the audience chuckled, Johnny corrected himself by saying, "I mean the Queen Elizabeth is in the lobby. . . . I don't where where in the world I got the lobby. . . . I mean, the Los Angeles Hobby . . . I mean, the Los Angeles Harbor."**

Cormick as shocking. "The first day I was there, I went into the bathroom and I was in the stall," he says. "Now McCormick's tall, like six-eight. He came in there, and I didn't know it. He just put his head over the door, and he was looking down at me. I looked up, and it was the most frightening sight I'd ever seen. I just screamed!"

And then there was the infamous *Tonight Show* streaking by McCormick in the early seventies. Remember the seventies? Ray Stevens's popular song "The Streak"? The nudie who traipsed across the stage on national television while David Niven was presenting an Oscar? Parading nude was a national rage—some called it an outrage.

For weeks Johnny had jokingly speculated that *The Tonight Show* might be streaked, and how funny that might be. On a Thursday night's taping, McCormick, clad in just a western hat and a Johnny Carson Halloween mask, ran across the stage in front of Johnny during the show. All he remembers is the particular, shrill screech of one woman, audible above all the audience's reactions, and how he's never heard the same high-pitched sound since. ("Maybe she recognized me.") Says McCormick of the stunt that ended up almost costing him his job:

*Naturally, from going to the set and looking at the cards, I knew the last joke. So I didn't interrupt the monologue. As soon as I heard the last joke—and I'm standing there on the side in an overcoat. Nobody took any notice of it because they never knew what I was gonna do anyway. I wanted this to be a* real *streak.*

*I thought it was a perfectly normal thing to do. I did not anticipate whatsoever that some New York lawyers at NBC would get all excited and annoyed by it. I ran toward the band, and the Johnny Carson mask I had on went over my eyes, and I couldn't see where I was running. People in the band said I was coming at them like a walrus or a rhino heading for them. A guy on the other side was holding the door. For a second, it gave me the terror of not being able to get out.*

Producers inserted a black band across McCormick's private parts, and the bit was aired. When the New York NBC offices saw what was on their television, they were blistered and moved to have McCormick dismantled from his prized position as Johnny's writer. Carson, knowing it was just a gag, went to the defense of McCormick. "I always appreciated that," McCormick says. "He's been a good friend."

Of the material that McCormick has handed Johnny, there was one instance when the routine didn't set well with the host, and the concept was ultimately turned down. It was during a period when a new pope was being installed as the Catholic Church's spiritual leader. "It was preempting NFL Football," McCormick remembers. "My idea was for Johnny to be the pope, and he would deliver the scores in Latin. Carson liked the skit, but because of certain reasons, we had to bow to that. He's pretty good at not doing religious stuff too often, unless it's a screwball cult or something.

"I think he's right," McCormick adds. "He stays away from ethnic and religious topics mostly. He razzes Democrats and Republicans. And mostly for the value of the humor. If it's funny, *do* it. He's one of the few voices of our times. Like Will Rogers. There's nobody like that anymore."

Greg Fields was a kid from Kentucky when he came out West with almost no money. He had a one-bedroom apartment with a bed that pulled out of the wall, when he blindly submitted some material to the head writer at *The Tonight Show* at the suggestion of a friend. After six weeks, someone called him back and said they thought his Carnacs and Floyd Turbo essays were good. "Let's hire him," Ray Siller said. He fit right in. "Johnny always thought, the worse you looked and the drunker you looked, the funnier you probably were," says Fields, whose appearance was admittedly sloppy. "Any writer who looks like he's got his life in order is probably not a very good writer. And as long as you can produce, you can dress and act like an idiot out here."

Fields began at a thousand-dollars-a-week salary, which nearly put him in shock when he found out, he says. He was still riding to work on a bus and gambling most of his savings away at the track, and none of his friends or family back home could actually believe he was writing for *the* Johnny Carson.

"He was my hero," Fields says. "In Kentucky especially, he's God." Fields admitted he was pretty naive when he began writing for his idol. One day at NBC, a studio worker asked him to help carry some heavy piping to the next soundstage. Being new, Fields thought he better assist, fearing a refusal might cause a commotion. Johnny's head writer, Ray Siller, spotted Fields and pulled him aside quickly.

"Hey, what the hell are you doin'?" Siller asked. "You work for Johnny, you know. You don't have to do heavy lifting!" Siller laughed as he walked away from the rookie. In essence, the writers were Johnny's boys. *He* could pick on them, but nobody else could.

Fields points out that writing for Johnny Carson was one of the best jobs in "town"—or Hollywood. It was a great place to begin, the salary was very nice, and almost always a graduate of the Carson comedy crew could go elsewhere and find a position—whether the departure was by his choice or Johnny's. In Fields's case, he left after nearly two years when Johnny was "cleaning house," he says. Since, he's written for shows such as *Solid Gold*, and the ill-fated *Pat Sajak Show* and later he wrote the story line for Rodney Dangerfield's hit film *Back to School*. He's now a senior writer for

Near Christmas one year, Johnny told the viewers: " . . . and now I'm going to read some letters from legitimate children . . . (audience laughed) . . . you know what I mean."

TV's *In Living Color*, where the humor is current but not as urgent as when he was employed by Johnny Carson.

He explained: "If there was nothing going on in the news, you'd see writers bullshitting, trying to come up with stuff. Pee-Wee Herman masturbating in a porno theater—every writer in town was on that. That's something to write about. It's the slow news times that kill you."

Oddly enough, Carson made no on-air comments about the 1991 Pee-Wee incident. During a commercial break in taping a *Tonight Show* when Pee-Wee news was still hot, Carson opened the field for questions from the audience. "What do you want to talk about, anything?"

The audience yelled out, "Pee-Wee! Pee-Wee!"

He hesitated, smiled, looked at Ed. The audience kept yelling "Pee-Wee!" Finally, McMahon sided with the audience. "Just one joke?"

Carson broke down. "Okay. But if you tell anyone I said this, I'll deny it. There's a few jokes going around. Evidently, Pee-Wee's gonna represent himself in court . . . . Because if he does, he thinks he can get himself off."

Carson's decision to confine Pee-Wee cracks solely to commercial breaks was a compliment to his editing skills. He *knew* every show, every host, every comedian would be offering jibes. And it happened, just like that. Carson was just about the *only* host to avoid the clichéd topic.

If the writers submitted Pee-Wee jokes, or any jokes that were omitted by Carson in the monologue, it was all right, says Fields. "The whole idea, like any show, is to please the guy with the ball and bat," he says. "Make him happy. And even if Johnny picked the jokes and they didn't do well, that was okay. Because this is the king picking them. This isn't Arte Johnson saying 'I don't like that.'"

Fields continued: "When I first got my job on *The Tonight Show*, I was twenty-four, and I used to think, Johnny never comes around. He never asks me to go have a drink. Johnny never calls me on the weekends. What an asshole! And then, I got out there the next few years and worked for every other star, and realize he's the nicest guy to work for. For as much power as he has, he could've busted everybody's balls, but he didn't really do it. He didn't abuse his power. And these other little Hollywood pipsqueaks really do it."

Nostalgia ripples through every word that Fields says. He's a Carson fan from way back, ever since his grade-school teacher wrote for Carson's autographed picture in the early 1960s and later presented little Greg with the photo as a gift. He's kept it all these years. Even when he worked for the man, he never updated that signature. He only met Carson and talked with him maybe ten times during his stay at NBC, and says he never walked into Johnny's personal office. But he's a fan through and through, with respect for Carson's stamina.

"He's been going out there every night," Fields says, "and it's like mental gymnastics. To see jokes at two o'clock and go out there at five? For a sixty-six-year-old man, it's unbelievable. So many others can't do it. Jay Leno's tried most of his jokes out six or seven times. Once he gets that job every night, it'll be a whole new ball game."

The end of Carson on *Tonight* means an end of an era for Fields, for America, and naturally, for Carson and his whole bunch. Johnny was quick with "Hey, I'm outta

During one of Johnny's monologues, someone in the audience yelled out to ask if his wife was at the show. Carson replied, "No, she only comes on anniversaries." The audience went wild at the unintended sexual overtone.

here!" jokes his last year, but almost as hasty in reminding audiences he's just retiring from the show. He isn't dying.

"I don't think people will realize how sad they'll be when the thing winds down," Fields says, referring to the show as an institution—a public property to be enjoyed each night. "It's the last vestige of show business. You can feel the five hundred people tense up and really get excited," he says of when the audience sits in anticipation of Johnny's coming out from the curtain. "Most of the audience have never seen him in person. I loved to stand by that curtain and just watch their faces. It's what show business used to be. When people came into town, they'd want to see a *real* show, done in an hour, and see the biggest star. This is the guy they've watched most of their lives."

# The Art of Bursting Bunkum

by Neil Shister

What I like best about Johnny Carson is what, in general, I like least about other people—his steadfast refusal to commit himself to virtually anything other than his own stagecraft, which, in its best moments, means stepping in and out of social confusion with equal parts impulsive abandon and icy detachment.

For what seems an untold number of years, Johnny Carson has made me laugh. (I don't date Carson in standard chronology, but rather by the phases of my life we've shared, and I can vividly recall several eras back rushing home from the college library to catch his monologue.)

He hasn't intellectually stimulated me, nor caused me to think new thoughts or see the world in a different light, but simply—and regularly—has made me laugh. Often out loud.

More than anything else that readily comes to mind, he has been the consistent presence in my adult life. It's not that I follow him devoutly. There have been huge stretches when I don't tune in, months when I don't watch. But he's always there to come back to, the way one resumes contact with a trusted friend, holding down the fort with irony that can salvage even the worst of days like a brandy nightcap.

In person, so tales go, Carson is sullen, reclusive, intensely private. He's given to spending time at parties barricaded in a corner, nervously tugging the knot in his tie. He has been through several marriages, is reputed to have once had a drinking problem, and can, on occasion, be positively surly.

I find none of this disconcerting. On the contrary, it adds to his on-camera charm, the fact that his unflappable, accommodating cool is masking a considerably less sociable nature. My Carson, the one who has peered forth at me in some intimate moments, is something of a rogue, one who speaks with slightly forked tongue but gets away with it because of his disarmingly innocent manner.

There is to Carson a quintessentially American quality, distilled no doubt from the Nebraska heartland he hails from. Years ago, in his six-bedroom Bel Air home hung a portrait of the man painted by Norman Rockwell. It was a perfect match: that idealist of the American scene portraying the televised embodiment of the ideal American personality, a title Carson has earned, if only through longevity.

That quintessential quality is, I'd hazard, cynical civility. It's a willingness to let each person speak his mind, coupled with an unwillingness to take all that is said at face value. The old Missouri "show me" stuff.

But Carson, to get back to his refusal to go public with his politics, doesn't debate on the air, doesn't force his guests to prove their points. In his monologues he scatologically scathes assorted newsmakers (in 1973 he mentioned that Richard Nixon was unworried about the gas shortage, adding, "That's understandable, of course—everything's *downhill* for him").

But he does this in such a random way that some shrewd observers regard his remarks as an astute barometer of public opinion, not the concerted assault of an identifiable ideologue.

No, what Carson does is puncture bunkum with deadpan humor of polished economy. In a moment of upward-rolling eyeballs or a startled shake of his head as if he were dozing off, he expresses stunned disbelief or disagreement. This is his nightly genius, this talent for building a laugh off an unwitting straight man seated on his right, while still maintaining the facade of the dutiful host displaying his best manners.

He makes conversation on camera the way, say, Picasso might have doodled: less as an end in itself than a prelude to something grander. In Carson's case, that means a topper, a joke spontaneously pulled out of the air that suddenly gives order to an unstructured dialogue. One doesn't watch Carson to hear what others have to

**Forever youthful, Carson's all-American boyish face, hazel eyes, and a natural sly smile combined with a relaxing demeanor have made him utterly magnetic with audiences.** *(from the author's collection)*

say (too often they tend to be show-biz glitter types of the most passing interest) but rather to watch Carson work.

Perhaps what finally most fascinates me about Carson is the certainty that I could never do what he does, to be so rigorously "on" over such a sustained length of time. He reminds me of how Joe DiMaggio has been described, a ballplayer of such raw talent that he could make the toughest plays look easy. Even when a line in the monologue falls flat, he sidles away from it with a hint of self-deprecation calculated to pan a comic payoff out of his own predicament.

Carson's is a singular presence on the screen. In his natty suits and trimmed haircuts, he represents, to me, the perfect corporate-type go-getter gone ever-so-slightly bad. He's intimately acquainted with the "system" and its self-effacing discipline—but clearly not of it, having escaped while never decisively turning his back on its decorum.

*Neil Shister is a former* Time *magazine correspondent and TV critic for* The Miami Herald. *He was publisher and editor of* Atlanta *magazine before accepting his current position as Vice President of the custom-publishing division of Hill and Knowlton, Inc., in Chicago.*

# 7

## Paging Johnny Carson

"It was so hot in Los Angeles today," states Johnny, weaving into a joke. . . . "How hot *was* it?!"

Ever wonder what happens to the people who shout out loud at Johnny during his monologue—*especially* during the monologue?

They are promptly and silently escorted out of the studio with no chance of seeing the remainder of the show. Cruel and unusual punishment, wouldn't you say? Much to Carson's chagrin, this popular retort, amended for any occasion, has become an instantaneous response to statements in his monologue over the years. And it's the responsibility of the dark sport-coat-clad NBC pages, happy with a smile, to scan the audience for the loudmouth with his hands cupped, and respectfully, but forcefully, yank the bloke from his spot. Sure, everybody wants to be heard on the air, later alerting friends and watching the show in anticipation of his brief howl. But try it on the Carson show, and the tube is the only way you'll see the action.

Playing bouncer for Johnny was one of the discouraging points in an otherwise desired position. The ultimate, however, was the actual appointment to work the show among the other chores.

"Five pages are in-house, instructed not to watch Johnny, don't watch the monologue, don't enjoy yourself," explains Ken Crosby, thirty, a former NBC page. "Just watch the audience. For any 'How hot was it?' or 'Whoop,' the culprit was ushered out. It happened at least two to three times a week."

On his first day paging a *Tonight Show* with the man whose name was in the title appearing as host, Crosby could hardly repress himself in expectation of catching his first glimpse of Carson in person. "I'm a celebrity freak and excited about seeing him," says Crosby of his second week at work. "Fred de Cordova came out and reminded the audience that Johnny had been away for two weeks and that he was back. Five, four, three, two . . . then the theme. Carson comes out from behind the curtain, and it was like a rock-concert-type thing. Everyone rose to their feet in a roar, yelling out. For a new page having anxiety about seeing Carson, it was frightening."

With the arrival of Arsenio Hall to Televisionland, audiences today are louder, more rambunctious, and eager to bellow and bark. "Ruder audiences," Crosby describes them. "People get rowdy. They're in town on vacation and some overtly run across the street to the A & O Liquor to get beer to drink while they wait in line. I'm five-foot-seven and I'm not an imposing page, but asking these frat buddies to leave the studio in silence was a bit unnerving."

One 1991 audience was so rude, it had Carson tongue-tied. Openly aggravated by

The American Dream: NBC pages Tamara Anne Fowler and Ken Crosby secretly pose at Johnny's desk for this personal snapshot after the show one evening when the set was dark. *(courtesy of Tamara Anne Fowler)*

one fan in particular, Carson looked up in exasperation and said, "Oh shut up!" delivering an "up-yours" arm gesture to the person. Pages could not zero in on the hooligan, and during the desk piece, which seemed to bomb that night, he once again loudly announced from the audience his opinion of the skit: "Stop, you're killing me!"

"It's a thought!" Carson countered. The audience roared. That night, even guest Bill Cosby, like a sassy schoolmarm scolding the class clown, playfully instructed the audience to apologize to Johnny for its collective rudeness. Indeed, it was a rare night for the fairly unflappable host.

Evenings such as this were jittery for pages like Crosby, who guarded his job with pride and competitiveness. He arrived in Hollywood in 1984 from his home in Hawaii, where he left "a prestigious position as cashier for Toys 'Я' Us." His passion for Johnny Carson and *The Tonight Show* ushered him to the job, which paid a meager $5.20 an hour and had a maximum service of eighteen months. If you were good, you received an extra month or two extension, he explains, but much of the glitter wore off after a year.

Approximately 130 people applied each month for the coveted entry-level position at NBC, said network officials. In 1991, the page system was thrown out, a victim of network cutbacks, but prior to that nearly fifty pages might be employed at once. The waiting list was extensive. Paging is a hybrid position, the responsibilities of which include: conducting the studio tour; ushering; and serving as guest-relations personnel, audience prompter, clerical worker, and often gofer. Sometimes you were sent on a "limo run," escorting a celebrity to the studio. Sixty percent of the training was for *The Tonight Show*, both in maintaining security and order, and handling the nightly mass of 450 ticket-holders who might have stood hours in the heat for their audience with the King.

The *Los Angeles Times* reported, "Pagedom began the climb to stardom for celebrities like Kate Jackson, Richard Benjamin, Steve Allen and Eva Marie Saint, as well as several top executives who have served as pages during the 51 years since the studio began the program in New York." Chris Elliot of *Late Night* fame, the late game-show host Bert Convy, and Regis Philbin also started careers as pages. Daily exposure to a major television studio was not only thrilling to these pages; they hoped it would prove a successful entrée into the network. Competitiveness among the pages has always been described as "fierce."

Peter Lassally, a former page who is the last in a string of producers for Johnny Carson, says he feels a special warmth for pages who approach him for advice. "I'm happy to talk to them and give expertise," Lassally told the *L.A. Times*. "It's a lot harder than when I was a page back in the 1950s. There was more opportunity to get into television because radio was still the big deal."

Being an NBC page could've meant bumping into Johnny Carson, Ed McMahon, or maybe Vanna White in the hallway, although Carson was labeled "strictly hands off." You might cross the path of producer Freddy de Cordova steering his personal golf cart (with a drink in one hand and a lovely female page in the passenger seat), zipping through the halls, or maybe you'd schmooze with a few celebrities visiting the studio that day.

"The job as a whole certainly had its pitfalls too," admits Crosby. "The tour was basically walking backward for an hour and showing people from the Midwest empty studios and trying to create some sort of magic that just isn't there in most cases. Foremost for me was doing *The Tonight Show*."

Experiencing the famed NBC tour was fun unless, unaware that it was the final voyage of the day, you purchased a ticket for the 3:30 P.M. "Death Tour." News studios had closed doors, and Studio One, housing *The Tonight Show*, was forbidden territory. "People just didn't get their money's worth, and [the pages] complained to NBC to cross off that tour, but they wouldn't," Crosby says. At a good time, however, you might see:

- The Mini-Studio, where you are shown a few basic camera operations and control-board techniques—all demonstrated by hired pages.

- Studio Four, where Elvis's 1968 NBC comeback special was taped (on June 27, 29, and 30, and aired December 3), and where Fred Astaire danced magic into his NBC specials.

- The *Wheel of Fortune* set.

- Studio Five, a smaller locale that includes the set for David Horowitz's *Fight Back* show.

- The KNBC news studio, Los Angeles's local NBC-TV affiliate, adjacent to the network's buildings.

Crosby notes one treat you *did* get on the Death Tour was a chance to see, up close, Johnny's car in parking spot number 1. "I'd tell 'em, 'I know *The Tonight Show* doors are closed, but I've got a treat for you folks . . . ,'" Crosby says, recreating his spiel. "'I really shouldn't be doing this, but come on out here.'

"By God, there would be Johnny's white Corvette, and the women would swoon," Crosby laughs. "The car was the 'saver' on those Death Tours. But anyone approaching the car to test the locks or touch it would quickly find us obedient pages throwing ourselves between the gawker and the car. It's much more important for you to lose a limb than let one of the people hurt Johnny's car."

For the sake of pure climax, most tours were led into an empty, chilly Studio One, to stare at *The Tonight Show* set with just a few dim lights shining above the desk and the orchestra area. "If you'll imagine, ladies and gentleman, in no more than three hours from now, through these doors that you are about to pass, Mr. Carson will arrive. . . . He

Actress Cybill Shepherd was quoted in a periodical saying she thought Johnny Carson was an interesting individual and that she'd love to have dinner with him. Carson invited the actress on the show and prepared an impromptu catered dinner (courtesy of the NBC commissary) with candles, china, and champagne. When Carson popped the cork on the champagne, it bubbled all over his desk; Shepherd took her linen, wiped the spill, and replied, "You should have spilled it on your pants, and I could have cleaned it up."

> Introducing a Sara Lee commercial, Johnny wondered if anybody had ever actually seen Sara Lee, and he joked that she was probably "some little alcoholic old lady in the Midwest who is half in the bag all the time." He was quickly made aware that the sponsor had named the bakery product after his young daughter and was not amused by Carson's jest.

will have along with him Mr. de Cordova, or an assistant, going over the show's events, and he will go through here and around right to this curtain." The page would explain the history of *The Tonight Show* and its New York roots. The story of Shelley Winters falling asleep while on the couch during a show would familiarize tourists with the boom mike that detected her snores. And if you were lucky enough to have tickets for the evening's taping, you stayed around the area and secured a place in line.

The militarylike operation of ushering in audiences for *The Tonight Show* was usually so smooth it ran like machinery, partly due to the behavior of the well-trained NBC pages. Some of them, confident and proud like the peacock on their blue blazer, are amicable and helpful. Other pages appear proud but a little too cocky, ready to ruffle the feathers of anyone who gets out of line. After the Persian Gulf War, a walk-through metal detector was installed, and a guard who peeked inside purses with a flashlight and observed bulging pockets was stationed right inside the entry door. Cameras have always been strictly forbidden, and audience members are instructed to take them back to their vehicles before entering the studio.

If you were the OIC (Outside in Charge) page, it was your job to keep the VIPs placated. Friends of staff or those with the show would be instructed to pick up their tickets at the guest-relations bungalow, where "tape and hold" seats in their name were kept. For those lucky enough to obtain these honored arrangements, preferred seating close to the stage was provided as well as the elimination of a wait in line. Just as scary as audience removal was the opportunity to hold the master clipboard and advise some ticket hopefuls that for some reason, their name was *not* on the list. Those claiming their coveted reserved seats approach the pages with an intense look on their face, as if they are prepared to have an audience with the pope. If their tickets are not there, a surge overcomes many of them, and veins in their neck start to bulge as they look as if they will wring the neck of the presiding page in their presence. Rants such as "You don't know who I am!" or "You'll never work in this town, you little shit!" could be heard, says Crosby. Persistent persons would want to "make some phone calls," inevitably inquiring about the nearby staff phone, which is reserved for emergencies. "What the hell . . . ?!"

Few complications halted any facet of *The Tonight Show* tapings, explains former page Tamara Anne Fowler. "I was there once when a little old lady had a heart attack during the taping," she says. "The show went on. It stops for almost nothing."

Fowler abandoned her berth at a Los Angeles ad agency, suffered a massive cut in pay, and moved back in with her parents at age twenty-five to accomplish her dream of paging *The Tonight Show*. Her goal: to pass the prize envelopes to Johnny during a segment of "Stump the Band." Alas, she never got the chance before her time was up. Another page, Herbie J. Pilato, aspiring actor, author, and celebrity, was pushed up in the ranks to serve for Carson. Fowler admits to being one of the more notorious pages for pulling pranks and deviating from decorum—the reason she supplies for her release from NBC.

Her favorite memory from the NBC experience was meeting Marlon Brando while on "screening-room duty." Brando was displaying a Super 8 reel of footage about his private island hideaway, pitching a documentary concept to network executives. "It was one of those days where nothing went right," Fowler recalls. "The film wouldn't stop flickering. Then no sound. Then the film broke and we had to tape it. One guffaw after another.

"At the end, another page and I were rewinding it, and I waited by the door to see Marlon Brando go by. He rounded the corner and came right in. He shook my hand and said thank you, but not sarcastically. He was huge and very imposing. I thought, of all the people to make mad. But he was very controlled and not a hothead."

Starstruck pages were usually treated to on-the-job sightings, a perk at work, they say. Page Ken Crosby, working an NBC Lucille Ball tribute, opened the door for an approaching Dean Martin, Frank Sinatra, and Sean Connery, bidding them "Have a nice evening, gentleman."

"We shall," Connery said. It wasn't often Matt Helm, Tony Rome, and James Bond exited the building at once, Crosby mused.

# By the Numbers

- Over **24,000** guests have appeared on *The Tonight Show*.

- When Johnny Carson began hosting *The Tonight Show* in 1962, his average nightly audience was almost **7.5 million** viewers; in 1972 it exceeded **11 million**; in 1978 it totaled **17.3 million**; and by 1992 more than **32 million** tuned in.

- In 1992, the number of NBC television affiliates airing Johnny Carson nightly: **212**.

- The show has undergone **7** set changes over the years.

- Over **212** different animals have been showcased.

- Johnny has asked over **200,000** questions of his guests.

- There are **465** seats in NBC's Studio One in Burbank.

- Between **200** and **300** ticket requests arrived daily for *The Tonight Show* in 1991.

- Most nights, Doc's band is a **16**-member ensemble.

- About **83** guest hosts have subbed for Johnny Carson.

- The Tonight Show has taken home **5** Emmy awards.

- Johnny Carson has clobbered **14** similar talk/variety show hosts in competition for the time slot.

- Nearly **3 million** people have attended *Tonight Show* tapings since Johnny Carson became host.

- About **850** different sponsors have participated in the financing of *The Tonight Show* over the years.

- More than **250,000** commercials have aired during breaks of *The Tonight Show Starring Johnny Carson*.

- Advertising rates on *The Tonight Show* were **$17,200** per minute in 1968, **$20,000** per minute in 1973. In 1991 the rate was **$35,900** for a thirty-second spot. For Johnny's final night, the cost was more than quadruple the norm.

- Johnny Carson has broadcast a little over **486,180** minutes on NBC. This translates to just over **8,103** hours on television. If you ran his shows back-to-back, it would equal **337** days (nearly one year) of continuous airtime.

- Johnny Carson hosted **3,641** *Tonight Show*s as of September 3, 1976 and **5,837** shows as of October 1, 1985; when he retires, Johnny Carson will have hosted about **6,603** different episodes with sidekick Ed McMahon.

Johnny marks his 14th anniversary, and the 3,641st first-run telecast, with a two-hour special in 1976. *(Personality Photos, Inc.)*

- Johnny Carson's first job was in 1949 at a Nebraska radio station where he earned **$47.50** a week.

- Johnny Carson's starting *Tonight Show* salary in 1962 was **$100,000** a year. His year's salary in 1991 has been estimated at **$20 million**. His current gross annual income is estimated to be **$40 million**.

- Carson's salary in 1991 worked out to be about **$2,380** for every minute he was on the air.

- Johnny Carson's last contract called for him to host **111** hourlong shows per year with fifteen weeks' paid vacation.

- Johnny Carson has been married **4** times (as of 1992).

- Ed McMahon shed a noticeable **42** pounds in 1990.

- *The Tonight Show* in 1991 reportedly accounted for about 15 percent (**$60 million**) of NBC's total revenue.

- NBC Research estimated that since Carson became the host of *Tonight*, his audience has totaled over **83 billion** viewers.

- During his last several years, Johnny Carson received between **500** and **700** letters a week all addressed personally to him in care of NBC.

# 8

# A Comic's Dream

## by Joe Rhodes

*AUTHOR'S NOTE: This is the story of a comic's tour de force on* The Tonight Show *in 1985. Writer Joe Rhodes and comic Anderson have been pals from Minnesota for ten years. Formerly on staff with the* Dallas Times Herald, *Rhodes is now a free-lance writer and a correspondent for* Entertainment Weekly *magazine living in Los Angeles.*

Louie Anderson heard his name and knew it was time to move toward the light. There was no more time to worry, no more time to dream. There was only time to straighten his tie and swallow hard, to catch a glimpse of the stagehand who was holding the gray curtain open, who was gesturing for him to go ahead.

He walked through the curtain, looked briefly to his right, and smiled at the scene that was just as he'd always hoped it would be. There was Johnny Carson, behind his famous desk, in front of his famous Hollywood backdrop, smiling and clapping his hands. Robert Blake, dressed in black and fingering an unlit cigarette, was in the guest's chair. And yes, on the sofa, there was Ed McMahon, clapping along.

Louie Anderson found his mark, two pieces of green tape stuck to the floor in the shape of a *T*, and positioned himself in front of the camera. To his left, Doc Severinsen was giving the signal to end the music, the generic brassy music they use for every new comedian. This time, though, the music sounded different to Louie Anderson. This time the music was for him.

"I could work the rest of my life touring in clubs, and tomorrow night more people will see me than in all those clubs put together," Louie had said the day before. "This is what every comic dreams of. It changes everything because for the rest of your life, wherever you go, they say, 'As seen on *The Tonight Show.*'

"Not many people get a chance like this—one night that can change their whole life."

The amateurs were everywhere, tables full of people who thought they were funny, waiting for their shot at making strangers laugh.

It was another take-your-chances Monday night at the Comedy Store, the legendary comedians' proving ground on Hollywood's Sunset Boulevard. Monday is open-microphone night, which means anyone who wants to make a fool of himself in public need only take a number and wait in line.

Most of the applicants were crowded in a back corner, a huddled mass of wretched

Louie Anderson, the stand-up comic who blew away Carson during his debut *Tonight Show* stint on November 20, 1984. *(courtesy of Louie Anderson)*

comedy refuse, laughing at one another's jokes, the only ones laughing in the room. Some of it was painful to watch, the feeble attempts at being funny.

They would go to the stage, one after another, always moving too fast, always fumbling with the mike, trying to get one laugh before their three minutes expired. One guy showed up with a two-by-four and said things like "I found this at a board meeting." One was doing Mary Jo Kopechne jokes. Another simply froze and uttered not a single intelligible word. He just stood there muttering, waiting for the light to shine on Eddie Cantor's portrait, the sign that his time was up.

It was an endless parade of half-wits and loudmouths, guys who thought they could get laughs just by saying dirty words and making faces. If, by some incredible accident, one of them uttered a line that was even remotely humorous, the crowd would go crazy. Mercy laughs.

But mixed among the pitiful amateurs, there are always a few people who know what they're doing, young comics who have come from other places, ready to take their shot at the big time. If you're going to make it as a comedian, this is where you have to start, taking a number and standing in line on Monday night at the Comedy Store.

That's what Louie Anderson did. He came to L.A. in September 1982, four years after he had taken a dare and gone onstage at a comedy club in Minneapolis, a cramped working-class bar called Mickey Finn's. He was a social worker at the time, a kid who'd grown up dirt-poor in a St. Paul housing project.

Louie was funny and he knew it, a 350-pound guy who could make fun of himself and everything around him. He was a hit the first time he took the microphone, and it wasn't long before he left social work behind. Deep down, he says, a comedian is what he'd always wanted to be.

After accomplishing all he could in Minneapolis, he took off for California. He planned to stay a year, and then, if he hadn't gotten on *The Tonight Show*, he'd go back to Minnesota. A year passed. He didn't get on. He stayed anyway.

He'd become a paid regular at the Comedy Store by February 1983, only six months after his arrival. He'd even gotten an early audition for Jim McCawley, *The Tonight Show*'s talent coordinator. But McCawley turned him down, said he wasn't ready. Louie swore he'd never audition for the show again.

"I was devastated," he said. "I'd been rejected, and I took it very personally. I'm immature. I think comics are immature people."

A few months later, abandoning his promise, Louie auditioned again. And he was turned down again. By then, though, he was getting plenty of work in comedy clubs on the West Coast and working as an opening act in Las Vegas for artists such as Neil Sedaka and Connie Stevens. So he stuck it out.

Finally, McCawley came through. He called Louie back for one more audition in mid-November and decided he was good enough.

"You're gonna get your show," he told him. "We'll do it in the next three or four weeks unless someone cancels."

The Friday after that conversation, Louie's phone rang. It was McCawley.

"You're doing it Tuesday," he said. "This Tuesday."

Louie calmly went over the specifics. He'd have seven minutes and would go on after Robert Blake. Fine, he said to McCawley, thank you very much. He then proceeded to call every human being he could think of.

"I don't care if I haven't talked to you in three years," he said to one long-distance friend. "Watch the show."

He had spent the weekend honing his act, working on the lines McCawley had liked, taping his club performances and playing them back against a stopwatch.

And now it was Monday night, the night before the big show, and he was in the midst of all the amateurs so he could try out his *Tonight Show* set for one last audience. A final dry run.

While he was waiting to go on, every comic in the back hallway was asking questions and giving advice. "Is Johnny gonna be there?" they wanted to know. "Do you get to sit down?" "What are you gonna wear?"

He was loving every second of it, basking in the glory, hamming it up, trying to pretend he wasn't nervous and doing an awful job.

"Do you think I need a haircut?" he asked. It was 11:00 P.M. "If you don't feel good about your hair, it makes a difference. I better get one tonight. If I can find the woman who cuts it for me, will you drive me over there? Great."

He did his set twice that night, the same jokes in the same order that he would do them for Carson and 18 million viewers in less than twenty-four hours.

"Sorry, I can't stay long," he said as he walked onstage "but I'm in between meals."

Small laughs. Very small. He was hurrying too much, rushing the punch lines, forgetting jokes. The lines were good, but his delivery wasn't. What should have been a seven-minute routine clocked in at under five.

"I went shopping today," he said. "What's this one-size-fits-all stuff?"

"Terrible crowd," he said, walking backstage.

He decided it was too late for the haircut and instead ending up going to Cantor's Delicatessen, a comedian's hangout.

"What time is it?" he asked after he'd ordered a Reuben sandwich.

"Twelve-fifteen," he was told.

"I'm gonna be on *The Tonight Show* tonight."

Louie lived in a one-bedroom apartment in North Hollywood, a town that is separated from the real Hollywood by hills, canyons, and money. There is no glamour in North Hollywood. It is an ugly, sprawling mass of prefab apartment buildings, construction-supply warehouses, and fast-food restaurants.

But it's cheap and it's convenient. A working comic's dream.

Louie's apartment—the walls covered in greenish Sheetrock, the bathroom cabinets stuffed with hotel towels—is crowded with comedy paraphernalia. There are old movie posters, ventriloquist dummies, a shelf full of props. The desk in the living room is covered with eight-by-ten promo shots of Louie, the paneling above the kitchen decorated with pictures of him arm in arm with assorted celebrities—Henny Youngman, Robin Williams, Mr. T, and Ray Charles.

"That's a good one, " Louie says. "He thought it was Gleason."

But Louie does most of his work from his bed. He's surrounded himself with every-

> Carson introduced singer and composer Mac Davis one evening by adding that Davis had to his credit "about a dozen songs in the top ten . . . "

thing he needs: telephone, answering machines, tape recorders, bookshelves. He stays in there for hours at a time. The day of his *Tonight Show* appearance, he stayed in there until nearly 2:00 P. M.

Friends called, telegrams arrived. Louie wandered into the shower and stayed there for almost an hour, listening to Prince's *Purple Rain* sound track over and over.

"Last night before I went to sleep, I went through the set in my head," he said, finally emerging from the bathroom only an hour before he was supposed to be at the studio. "I also had this dream that every bad thing I ever did in my life, Johnny had a list of it."

He seemed jumpy, a little disoriented. He couldn't find his socks. He said he was fine.

"I'm not nervous," he said. "I'm excited."

The taping didn't start until 5:30 P.M., but Louie wanted to get to NBC's Burbank Studios, a half hour away, by 4:00.

"I want to get there early," he said, "so I can see where I'm supposed to stand."

After the show, Louie would have to go directly to the Burbank airport and catch a flight to Las Vegas, where he and some other Comedy Store regulars were appearing at the Dunes Hotel. So now, there was a mad rush to pack his bags, to get everybody in the cars and caravan over to NBC.

The back-entrance security guards found his name on the list and waved the whole gang through, pointing out the proper parking area, very near Johnny's sparkling white Corvette. Everybody was piling out when Louie made a sickening sound.

"Oh God," he said. "I've left my suit at the apartment. The one I was going to wear on the show."

He wasn't nervous. Just excited.

One carload of comedians went back to retrieve the suit and Louie found his dressing room, a small paneled cubicle with a dressing table, a plaid sofa, a TV monitor, a coffee table, and a bathroom.

"Who was in here for the last show?" someone asked the security guard.

"Lee Meriwether, I think."

Louie's name was printed on a card that was fastened to the door and decorated with *The Tonight Show* logo. "I'm gonna save that," he said.

He asked the guard if he could walk onto the set. "You're the boss tonight," he was told, and wandered past the curtains into the empty studio.

"This is it," he said, looking up at the five hundred blue seats, turning to take in Johnny's desk, the couch, the cameras, the bandstand. "This is history."

He walked to Carson's star, the place where he stands to deliver his monologues, and stood there for a while, not saying anything.

By 4:45 the guys were back with the suit, and the tiny dressing room was filling up with friends, most of them nervously chewing on vending-machine pretzels.

"Nice place," one of them said. "Think we ought to knock on the door and see if Blake's in there?"

"No," Louie blurted. "Don't do that. Don't start acting like jerks."

Then he went to the bathroom.

Comedians kept showing up, Comedy Store regulars who'd done *The Tonight Show* themselves and were there to help Louie through his first time, sort of like a comedy support group.

"Louie, it's an easy room," said Bill Maher, a young comic who'd done the Carson show a dozen times and who had just signed to star in his own sitcom. "It's the easiest room you'll ever play."

"You won't sit down unless you go long," Maher told him. "If you go long, they can't bring out the third guest, and you get a freebie sit."

Louie was looking into the mirror. "I'm glad I didn't cut my hair," he said. "It looks just right."

At five-thirty, as the show started, they tried to turn on the monitor but couldn't figure out how to get it to work. The monologue was over before the picture came on. Johnny and Ed were on the couch by then, doing a bit about McDonald's selling its 50-billionth hamburger.

"Ohh," Louie said. "That should be my opening joke."

"Just wait," Maher told him. "Listen to this. You don't want to step on his routine."

Carson was rattling off statistics about McDonald's using 435 cows' worth of beef a day and 32,000 pounds of pickles.

"I should walk out there and say I was just at McDonald's," Louie said, "and all those statistics have changed."

"Don't do it," Maher warned. "Stick to the script your first time."

"You're right," Louie said. And he went to the bathroom.

It was 6:00 P.M. when the knock came. It was McCawley, the talent coordinator, ready to escort Louie to the backstage area. After the next commercial, Louie was on. They went down the back hallway together, turned right, and disappeared behind the curtains.

The pack of comedians made a mad dash through the green room, which isn't green at all, almost trampling Selma Diamond, who was to be the show's third guest. They were headed for the tunnel, the area behind the main camera, a place where they could watch Louie live, without a monitor, without having to peek through a curtain.

The commercial ended. Carson put out the cigarette he had been smoking while he was talking to Robert Blake off-camera. The spotlights were trained on the gray curtain, the stagehand standing behind it, out of sight.

"And now," Johnny Carson said, "will you welcome, please, Louie Anderson." This time the music was for him.

"I can't stay long," Louie said, coolly scanning the crowd as the music faded. "I'm in between meals."

It was like an explosion. The laughter rolled down like a wave. And it was his opening joke. Maher had been right. The easiest room he would ever work. Louie took the chance.

"I just got back from McDonald's," he said. Maher winced. The whole tribe of comedians, by then nearly a dozen, held their breath. "And all those statistics have changed."

Another roar. And Carson was bent over. Laughing.

"I've been trying to get into this California lifestyle," Louie was saying, as calm as he could be. "I went to the beach the other day, but every time I'd lay down, people would push me back into the water."

Every joke was perfectly timed, every punch line smoothly delivered. Louie did double takes. He waited for the applause, which came often. They were in the palm of his hand. He had a series of jokes about trying out for the Olympics, about how he drove the pole vault into the ground and straightened out the uneven parallel bars, and here it comes, the big one.

"Broad jump?" He waited for the beat. One. Two Three. "Killed her."

Another roar. Carson, the master himself, was pounding on his desk he was laughing so hard. Louie had scored beyond his wildest expectations. It was a fairy tale.

The last joke was followed by a thunderous ovation Louie acknowledged like a heavyweight fighter who'd just delivered a knockout punch. He turned, finally, and went back through the gray curtain. But the applause didn't stop.

And then, something that never happens. Carson called him back for another ovation and came over to shake Louie's hand.

"Did you see that?" one of the comics gasped. "Johnny never comes over like that. That's as good as it gets."

Louie took the extended hand and leaned forward, whispering into his idol's ear.

"Thank you," he told him, "for making a dream come true."

After the show, the dressing area was like a World Series locker room, all backslaps and war whoops. It all went too fast. There was Peter Lassally, the show's director, coming back to tell Louie that Johnny wanted him to do some concert dates with him, and then, the man himself.

"Helluva good spot," Carson said. "You were funny as hell. I'll have you back whenever you want."

Louie went to the bathroom.

There was not much time for parking-lot euphoria. There was that plane to catch for Vegas, but Louie's life had changed. All in seven minutes. He was thirty-one years old, and he knew nothing would ever be the same again.

Carson left in his white Corvette, McMahon took a limo. And finally, Doc Severinsen wandered into the parking lot.

"Hot stuff, Louie," he said. "A beautiful set."

Louie Anderson said someting about his dad, how he was a trumpet player, too. He

> When Zsa Zsa Gabor guested on the show with Johnny one night, she was sitting in the chair with her Persian cat in her lap. She said, "Johnny, would you like to pet my pussy?" Johnny said, "Sure, if you move that damn cat out of the way!"

blurted it out, just something to say, anything. The night suddenly felt so unreal, too much like the dream he'd had for so long.

"See you soon," Severinsen said, climbing into his car. "Undoubtedly, see you soon."

# Carson's Comic Criteria

After the comic's debut . . .

1. If the camera doesn't move back to Johnny to get a shot, or an expression, and precedes directly to a commercial—the comic's probably not invited back.

2. If Johnny's smiling, delivers an "okay" gesture to the comic, and just says, "We'll be right back," the comic did all right.

3. If Johnny's laughing still and says "He's funny" or "She's funny," or "Good stuff," repeating the comic's name—the comic's sure to be invited back.

4. If Johnny spontaneously invites the comic over to the couch, the comic is in pretty damn good shape. He was a hit.

5. If Johnny's on the floor pounding his fist and crying with laughter, you might see that comic guest-hosting the show next Tuesday night.

# Little Blacklist

**Comedian John Byner performs a parody of Carnac the Magnificent on his syndicated TV show *Bizarre*. (from the author's collection)**

If you had to name just three of Mr. Carson's mannerisms, you could do it. Over the years, Johnny Carson's little idiosyncrasies, quirks, and trademarks have become so intimately familiar to the viewing audience that anyone could be identified silently mocking Johnny by a mere hand gesture. This characteristic shtick mounted over the years. Merv Griffin, guesting with Carson once, said that impressionist Rich Little counted twenty-eight Carson "tics."

"He came out once and did a whole bunch of things, and I watched it and went crazy," Carson responded.

Rich Little confirms the number. He even performed his Carson shtick on *The Tonight Show* when guesting with Johnny, and it broke up the host. "He has an awful lot of mannerisms, and I use them when I imitate him," Little says of his nightclub act, which includes Carnacs and comebacks. "It gets a great reaction. I did my impression of him on his show all the time. He used to laugh. He seemed to like it. We had a great rapport there, and then suddenly it stopped."

Carson may feel that imitation is not a sincere form of flattery, but rather mockery. Many comics have "done" competent illusions of Johnny: John Byner, John Roarke, Dana Carvey. Whether Carson has expressed displeasure in these portrayals is not known; Carson's no stranger to the impression game either. His own highly accurate and amusing impression of Ronald Reagan was actually praised by the former president, and the actor-turned-politician even inscribed a picture of Carson doing Reagan to Johnny as a gag.

Rich Little, one of the first to get a near-perfect handle on the Carson mannerisms and distill them into an act, has run into Carson socially ("and he's always friendly, and smiley and polite," Little says), but the impressionist re-

The "Spittin' Images" puppet of Johnny Carson.

mains mystified over his status as a "no book," which he was stamped fifteen years ago. "People think I still do the Carson show, but it's been a long time. We had a falling-out, and I really don't know the reason," Little confides. "It just stopped. They say they don't book impersonators on the show anymore."

Little guest-hosted the show for Carson about a dozen times and says the exposure was terrific for his career. Little invited some of his favorites on the show like Jimmy Stewart and Jack Benny, and, of course, matched voices and wits.

"I think as soon as Johnny leaves, hopefully I will get back on the show," he says. "Until that group, you know, Freddie de Cordova and all, [goes] I don't think I'll get on at all. I *know* I won't. I'll be glad when he's gone."

Reminded that there's a rumor about a "little blacklist" looming over the talent coordinators, Little confirms its existence and adds, "Oh, it's quite a big list."

Alf imitates Carnac the Magnificent in an episode titled "Tonight, Tonight" of the NBC sitcom *Alf. (courtesy of Warner Brothers Television and Alien Productions)*

# 9

# Television's Parade of Humanity

## Grand Marshall, Johnny Carson

## by John Lofflin

*" Television is our culture's principal mode of knowing about itself. "*
—Neil Postman

Communications theorist Neil Postman, in a cranky but provocative argument against television and its effect on society throughout the century, asserted that television is our "culture's principal mode of knowing about itself." He offered that insight without apparent reference to *The Tonight Show Starring Johnny Carson*, although he could not have failed to recognize that for thirty years *The Tonight Show* has, in fact, told us more about our culture than any theoretical tract (except perhaps the rantings of that wild Frenchman Alexis de Tocqueville, who visited our shores in the early 1800s). In fact, *The Tonight Show* has often told us more about our culture than we wanted to know.

Through it all, Johnny Carson has been the narrator of our story. Tune in almost any weeknight since 1962, and you'd find him presiding over a parade of cultural clues fairly begging to be noticed: actors and actresses with bits of film to sell; writers as diverse as wry Calvin Trillin and mischievous Henry Miller, sometimes with books fresh off the press to promote, less often armed with nothing more than their public personae; musicians with music to perform and sell who were, coincidentally, awful interviewees; athletes and jugglers; zookeepers; health nuts; starlets at one end of the fame spectrum and the great washed-up at the other; comedians and psychologists—psychologists were often unwittingly funnier; politicians (one must guess they have always been the easiest guests to obtain); heroes; and fools. Each spoke to us with his dress and his manner as much as with words that were often muttered away into the darkness of the rooms in which we watched. Some were newly in love and it showed in their eyes, others so bored with life that even the prospect of being seen by 6.4 percent of the nation was not enough to shake them awake.

When hemlines slid up, *Tonight* viewers were the first to notice. When dress shirts were worn open instead of buttoned and tied, *Tonight* viewers were there. When dress shirts disappeared altogether in favor of T-shirts worn under twelve-hundred-dollar

The *New York Times:* "probably no performer in the modern era has had as much impact on style trends as Johnny Carson." *(from the author's collection)*

Johnny Carson's line of apparel popularized many fashions in the United States. In the 1970s, when Johnny began wearing turtleneck shirts, the fashion raced across America. *(courtesy of Steve Randisi)*

An RCA Television ad introducing glorious color television in 1965. The ad was naturally run in color. *(courtesy of Steve Randisi and RCA Corporation)*

sport coats, *Tonight* viewers were there. Also, when it became permissible to speak certain words in public, *Tonight Show* viewers were among the first to hear. When it became fashionable to speak of a live-in lover as one would a husband or wife, *Tonight* viewers heard, as they heard when it became possible to speak of gay friends in less than a whisper, to criticize matter-of-factly all elites of government, to point matter-of-factly to waste and pollution, to laugh easily at the silliness of all tradition and ritual. It is hard from this vantage point in history to remember a time when private conversation, let alone *public* conversation, did not permit such discussion, but rest assured that time does not predate *The Tonight Show.*

It wasn't the Brooklyn Dodgers moving to Los Angeles that told us the cultural center of the nation had gone west. It was 1972 and Carson moving *The Tonight Show* permanently to the City of Angels that did it. Carson has said it was easier to do his show there, closer to guests, better equipment. It was also warmer and friendlier there, leisure suits were just being fitted, and New York was about to go broke. New York was home to the dark humor of Woody Allen; California to the joys of Steve Martin. New York was *Looking for Mr. Goodbar.* California was *American Graffiti.*

What we have seen, even from the city that would make a good student union for Clown College, has not always been good. It was on *Tonight* that we first saw with our own eyes how detached and greedy our entertainment idols had become. Perhaps they had always been such scoundrels; it was *Tonight* that brought them into our living rooms. We often felt the urge to ask them to leave. It was also on *Tonight* that we saw those entertainment icons come to grips finally, though perhaps superficially, with most of the fears we shared. We heard them admit addictions, we heard the baby boomers' angst over having put off childbearing too long, we heard badly disguised jokes about divorce and emotional impermanence.

And yet, we never had the feeling Carson intended such. Unlike the slimy schools of pseudorighteous afternoon and morning talk shows that swim through the nineties in Carson's wake, we never tuned in to *The Tonight Show* expecting to learn, expecting to be shocked, expecting to be outraged, expecting to be mystified. Imagine the poor working stiff who tunes in to Sally Jessy Raphael for a moment's respite while he ties his shoes in the morning, only to see a panel consisting of four obese women dressed like belly dancers and four obese men dressed *only* in boxer shorts—well, not only in boxer shorts, one wearing a bow tie, another wearing a black cowboy hat and carrying a rope—discussing God knows what with a studio audience that seems to be keeping its raging emotions only barely under control. *The Tonight Show Starring Johnny Carson* was never, even at its most tasteless, so rotten.

In fact, it has always been Johnny Carson's flappability that most assured us. While humanity paraded past his desk through thirty years of cultural upheaval, the same Johnny Carson tapped his pencil, straightened his tie, panned for the camera. Researchers will long debate what he represented to his audience, but let them begin with these notions. He was, first, Nebraska to the core. Middle American. Decent. Caring. Befuddled. Romantic. Sensual. Capable of temper and sulk. Capable both of understatement, and, like most of us, of dancing beneath a lampshade at a party of friends. Contrast that to almost any image you hold of entertainers, of Hollywood or New York, of the culturally hip or conservatively dour. So strong is this persona, that we have often cringed when Johnny was embarrassed by a woozy guest or a starlet bent on displaying her entire charms. His has been the role of the permanent aside, of the narrator who simply told the story, without rancor, without accent or polemic, but not without passion or taste.

That is, perhaps, a particularly appropriate role for a narrator of American culture. American society is, after all, a society in which the distinctions between highbrow and lowbrow are constantly tested, in which change moves so rapidly that good manners must be chronicled daily lest they be obsolete by the time they are published. A certain lightness of step and balance are needed in this always unfinished society. Carson has had that step.

Johnny's first appearance in front of the multicolored curtain from home-base Studio One in Burbank, California, was on May 1, 1972. *(Globe Photos)*

Is it too much to say that across all these difficult years, he has been a great balm to the queasy stomach this society has so often produced? Political scientist Murray Edelman has pointed insightfully to the many ways our entertainment and news industries reassure us about our world. If we have watched the nightly news, we are now reassured that we know all a citizen needs to know about the day's activities. Election night coverage reassures us the battle was a fair one, the best man won, and we will not wake in the morning to tanks in the streets. Television comedies reassure us that couples of the opposite sex can live together without sin (*Mork & Mindy, Three's Company*); that single women can function properly in bastions of maleness like broadcast newsrooms (*Mary Tyler Moore*); that blacks can move into the middle class without losing their blackness (*The Jeffersons*); that violence in the pursuit of good is always justified and fun (*The A-Team, I Spy*, and others too numerous to list); that a sense of neighborhood is still possible in America (*Cheers*); that our roots are deep, our old values better, the common sense of the common man, whether he hails from the hills or the ghetto, is always superior (*The Fresh Prince of Bel Air, The Beverly Hillbillies*).

Most reassuring of all for three decades has been *The Tonight Show Starring Johnny Carson*. When the Vietnam War was raging in the jungles, and protestors were raging in the streets, Carson still walked through the curtain to cheers and laughter. It is often said that former president Lyndon B. Johnson worried that if he had lost (Walter) Cronkite, he had lost the war. However astute, Johnson probably missed the point. When Carson's monologues finally found humor in the war's follies, Johnson had unmistakably lost the war. Not that Carson was ever political. He simply made it safe to disagree.

In a 1979 interview with *Rolling Stone*, Carson seemed to see both sides. First, he said, ". . . I always look at myself as an entertainer. So it has bothered me for a while that we would get a little flak from the critics saying we're not doing anything 'deep.' *That's not the idea.*" Then he added: "I think some of the material we've done on political things is some of the best material on the air. And it does get a strong reaction—especially in the political arena. We sense the mood of the country very quickly."

Again, Carson seems best at staying within himself, playing to his strength. And, as he says, he knows his audience, and his audience is free with its opinion of him. He walks a fine line when his humor is political, but it is a line few other comics even see, let alone respect. In the same interview, he illustrated the line with the problems of House Ways and Means Committee chairman Wilbur Mills.

"When Wilbur Mills was in trouble with the infamous Fanne Foxe and the Tidal Basin thing, it was funny until people found out he was an alcoholic. And then you knew immediately to stay away from it, because you were taking advantage. . . ." That is a sensibility few others with power in American television seem able to grasp.

Never, however, has Carson given us the sick feeling in the pit of our stomach that some news stories have, that the world would never be the same in the trough of crisis. Edelman says that when the news gets most frightening, we say to ourselves about television programming (Carson is the most obvious example) that "if it is really as bad as it seems, they would cancel these shows." A viewer of the Johnny Carson Show may well have said to himself a half-dozen times since 1962, "If things were as bad as they seem to be, would Johnny be smiling? Would his tie be straight, his collar crisp? Would he be making jokes, teasing with Ed and Doc, interviewing the empty-headed? Nooooo."

The idea could be pushed too far, but certainly there is some instruction in the notion that the earliest antecedent to *The Tonight Show* in this century is the Chautauqua circuit that flourished before radio and vaudeville took away the nation's attention.

The Chautauqua circuit had both religious and social roots in the late 1800s. At Chautauqua Lake in northwestern New York, Methodist faithful gathered on summer weekends for music, Scripture, and Christian education. As political scientist James David Barber puts it: "Before long, in

Johnny lets his feelings show on May 12, 1984. *(Personality Photos, Inc.)*

that Victorian age, the founders of the program worried that the Devil might be lurking among the young people who were strolling at their leisure along the twilight shore. To fill their time, lecturers—not all of them ordained—were brought in. As night follows day, the founders progressed from modesty to ambition: they sought a star speaker ..."

Their stars were not unlike a modern Carson lineup, at least in occupation. Barber says the first star was none other than President U. S. Grant, and although sitting presidents have been outside Carson's reach, the list of entertainers, like Edwin Booth and Jenny Lind, would have been well within Carson's grasp; as would Barnum's midget "General Tom Thumb," writers like Charles Dickens (who, Barber reports, made a quarter-million dollars on the Chautauqua circuit in just two years), and Mark Twain.

In essence, the Chautauqua circuit was designed to lift the soul. It began as a religious experience and joined vaudeville and radio as general escape. When the Chautauqua circuit spread out from New York to the other shore, it often involved a full night's entertainment. After the parade from the railroad platform, Barber says, onto the stage would march the "'World Famous Bohemian Orchestra' in their colorful costumes, led by Mr. Giuseppi Bartolotta, sporting a large dark mustache, to sing 'Silver Threads Among the Gold.' Then perhaps after a rousing xylophone rendition of 'Funiculi, Funicula,' came the lecture, the educational centerpiece."

The centerpiece shared several important elements with the Carson formula. First, as Barber points out, the speaker sought "a strategy of least objectionable programming: nothing risque, nothing vulgar, nothing too disturbing." That meant no preaching, no Bible-thumping, no fire and brimstone. Political speakers came out in favor of democracy; reformers, Barber says, were generally against sins committed on other continents or, at least, in other cities. Speeches were short, sweet, happy, and inspirational. Speakers knew well they would be followed by a girl who played piano and trombone simultaneously, "or the 'Anvil Chorus' perform[ed] on real anvils in the dark, as electric sparks showered around."

It has always been Carson's genius, like the genius of those who once managed Chautauqua shows, to understand his audience so thoroughly, so innately, as to rarely produce an unhappy guest. More precisely, it has been his genius to understand *the setting* in which his audience partakes of *The Tonight Show.* It is, he once said, a show people watch between their toes.

*The Tonight Show* occupies a special setting in our lives. It is seen in the shank of the evening in most places. Those who must be at their posts by 8:00 A.M. watch it almost certainly as the final act of the day (well, *almost* certainly). In Nebraska, for instance, the evening's drama and comedy have finished, the local news is over, the weather and sports recorded, modest plans for the morrow made. Then, at no later than 10:36 P.M., the familiar theme music rises, and invariably the next thought is who will

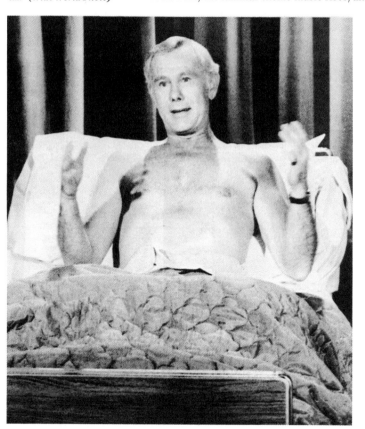

Beginning his seventeenth season, Johnny Carson was wheeled out by propman Jack Grant to deliver the monologue from a bed. "I thought I'd try something new," he said. "People seem to catch me while they're in the horizontal position, so now I thought I'd do the monologue while I'm horizontal." *(Wide World Photo)*

host tonight's session and who will guest. ("To guest," in fact, probably entered the language as a verb in the wake of the Carson show.) In most traditional households, children below the age of fifteen are doubtless in bed; the cottage may be still and quiet for the first time since alarms went off sixteen and a half hours earlier.

A certain demeanor is demanded of a visitor at that hour. The core audience of *The Tonight Show* is not watching it on televisions perched on shelves above long oak bars. It is an audience much more interested in a hot toddy of entertainment than a Fuzzy Navel.

A visitor at that hour ought not to be bombastic or loud. He ought not to raise great issues or great fears, even if he offers great solutions. He ought not to preach or gloat, or wring his hands, however righteously. If he offers a joke, and well he should, it must offer a mild laugh, it must be enlightening instead of disturbing, simple not complex. This is no time for rancor and angst, for the weird and disturbing tales that drive the daytime

talk shows. This is a time for Charles Nelson Reilly and Tony Randall; for vulnerable moments with Burt Reynolds; for Tony Bennett not Jimi Hendrix; for Dr. Carl Sagan, not Dr. Hunter S. Thompson.

In the *Rolling Stone* interview, Carson was clear about his vision of the audience: ". . . television is an intimate medium," he said. "I'm not conscious when I use the camera. I know it's there. I use it like another person and do a reaction at it—lift an eyebrow or shrug or whatever."

Later in the interview, sounding more like Dr. Marshall McLuhan than a talk-show host, he elaborated on his theory of television and television humor. "When NBC put on 'NBC Follies' years ago, they spent a lot of money building a proscenium stage, and they had these girls coming down in Ziegfeld-like costumes, and it didn't work because that essentially is Broadway and Hollywood—and TV is still an intimate type of thing, basically. Take the obligatory dance numbers they have in Broadway. . . . You see twenty

Burt Reynolds displays his mother's scrapbook in 1985 of his career highlights in newsprint. The appearance was at the peak of tabloid accusations that the actor was diagnosed as having AIDS. Reynolds denied it vehemently and said he felt good. *(Personality Photos, Inc.)*

Actress Dyan Cannon was a guest one night, and Johnny attempted to illustrate their close friendship, saying he had a "deep, penetrating relationship with her." Needless to say, the audience erupted.

dancers come out with a huge production number. It's really a filler to get ready for the next sketch or whatever. TV doesn't need that. Ed Wynn told me years ago about girls on television: he said 'What's sexy about a three-inch girl?' The point he was making was that when you see them on Broadway and they come down onstage and they're bigger than life, that's one thing. When you see them on television, it's often pointless and unimaginative. . . .

"To me, it's still the *performance* on TV that is most important. The personality is more important than all of the dance numbers and the big production things. I've always thought those things have been kind of lost on television, because they ignore the automatic *focus* that TV provides."

That focus is a two-way street. For viewers, the focus of television is always sharp. In television there are few long shots of bicycles a mile away on dirt roads, few characters dissolved from focus or dissolved into focus. There are no stage wings to which a viewer might be distracted. And from the performer's view, the focus of the audience ought also to be sharp. Little ambiguity is tolerated in television performances. The audience is out there, in its home, staring in, and nothing less than precisely drawn characters and inevitable plots will do.

Because, this, for God's sake, *is* our bedroom of our home in the last minutes of our day. It is no wonder so many others, who did not understand the setting, have come and gone from competing time slots. Whom would *you* invite to your bedroom door for the last conversation of the evening as the cicadas sang—Johnny Carson or Joe Pine?

While Johnny has always been the perfect guest, *his* guests have not always shared his mission. Many have seemed all too eager to shock, allowing black lace dresses to ride up nearly to their chins—or so it seemed—or holding forth with a series of words that would almost certainly be bleeped from rebroadcast. More often than not, the on-the-air Johnny Carson was not pleased, and he showed it, in gentle, subtle ways. Rarely has he been offensive in our homes, rarely has he insulted his guests, pushed them to reveal more than they wanted, milked their misfortunes for sensation.

In every mode of entertainment, there has been a man or woman for the season. Mark Twain seemed to understand perfectly what Chautauqua-goers wanted, the same way he understood what joy a frog could bring to the floor of a country church on Sunday morning. Franklin Delano Roosevelt seemed to know perfectly what radio listeners wanted to hear as they waited for him to announce the end of the Depression, and later, that the Germans had been routed. Orson Welles and John Huston, as well as Steven Spielberg, seemed to understand perfectly how the movie screen ought to tell its story in their eras, what behavior would be most appropriate when the curtains parted. And, of course, Johnny Carson has been the perfect narrator for the tiny glass screen that has adorned our living rooms, the electronic window on our world.

# Johnny: The Poor Man's Analyst?

**❝ But there is proof enough that, if greatly conceived, the popular arts can derive strength from a massive popular base and can reach the many by reducing themselves to simplest elements—that is, to their broadest humanity. ❞** —Max Lerner, Social Anthropologist

Johnny Carson has always helped obscure the difference in modern society between high culture and low culture. Not only has he done it by mixing the performances of Garth Brooks with those of Luciano Pavarotti, but also by producing a nightly television show that borders on art, at least by the standards established for television.

That he reached a massive audience is not the point. That he reached it with consistently polished and often excellent fare *is* the point. The popular culture has produced tons of schlock across this busy century, but Carson, even at his Mighty Carson Art Players worst, was not part of it. He may have reached a little lower than the Smithsonian, but he did manage to harvest the fruits of the popular culture with style.

If Carson is indeed following in the footsteps of the Chatauquans, he has gone them, and virtually every other entertainer, one better. Often overlooked in criticism of *The Tonight Show* is the fact that it is done every weeknight fifty-two weeks of the year. There are, of course, others in radio and television who are as regular as the sunset, but most, until recently, were in news. Today (no pun intended), mornings and afternoons are peppered with shows structured like *The Tonight Show*, or structured like a loose combination of *The Tonight Show* and an informal newscast. But few of those endeavor to bring viewers such a demanding array of humor and entertaining conversation every single day.

The demand, in fact, for something special every night—and supplying that does seem to be *The Tonight Show*'s aim—is daunting. Name one other comedian who has faced a television audience, monologue in cheek, more often than Carson. It seems perfectly logical to believe that he has told more jokes to more people than any other laughsmith ever. Yet he has never seemed to tire of the job. When he stands in front of the curtain and looks into the camera, his look is fresh and young, always, and he actually seems excited to have been invited into our homes. In an era when shortstops who can't hit their weight are paid a million dollars a year to look altogether bored by the seventh inning, Carson's enthusiasm is a wonder.

His sense of wonder is also important to the sense of the world we collectively share as a society. Who has not experienced some awful trauma—the death of a parent, a divorce, a lost job—and not turned ultimately to Carson for healing? He is, in an odd sense, the poor man's analyst. He doesn't listen and he doesn't offer advice, but he is solace and he is always there. The world will go on, he says with his presence, with his natty suit and his Nebraska smile. The heart might be breaking, but Carson's warm glow persists, promises a night of unchallenging entertainment (even if one is too distraught to pay attention), and promises to return tomorrow.

Forgive us if he means more than logic argues. Forgive Douglas Ward Kelley for suggesting in a 1978 article in *Argosy*—setting down in print what many of us had said to ourselves in jest—that Johnny Carson "would make a fine president." Kelley's logic went like this:

"... Johnny Carson is one of the best known men in America. His quick wit and positive demeanor have kept him at the very top of his profession longer than anyone could have predicted. ... There is something solid about him, a unique vigor. ... He is the greatest entertainer in America. ... " Floyd Turbo for president? Not really so farfetched if you recall that the Republican party nominated a former actor the following year.

Carson can, then, be forgiven if nothing very important happens during his ninety minutes. Who wants the promise of a glimpse of Al Capone's treasure when he turns on *The Tonight Show*? Not its faithful. They will settle for an increasingly rare "Stump the Band." Norman Mailer once said that the best of television rode the edge of a sinister meanness, like the 1950s Mike Wallace interview show *Night Beat*, on local television in New York, or perhaps Joe Pine in the 1960s or Geraldo Rivera today. But that just illustrates how young both television and Mailer were when he made that statement.

The suggestion has been offered many times—but not by Johnny Carson, who wants to stick with the comedy and entertainment business. *(Wide World Photo)*

William Reynolds of St. Catharines, Ontario, decided to produce a line of portable toilets with a catchy phrase. Sometimes referred to as "Johnny on the Spot," this new line of porta-potties were to be titled, "Here's Johnny."

Carson, upon learning of the marketing scheme, investigated the matter, and the registrar of trademarks decided to allow Reynolds to use the trademark for his business of renting portable outhouses. Carson appealed.

The Associated Press reported on March 12, 1980, that a Federal Court of Canada judge ruled that "Here's Johnny" is just too readily associated with Johnny Carson and *The Tonight Show* to be allowed as a trademark for portable toilets. Before rendering the decision, Justice Patrick Mahoney had accepted as evidence a random survey "in which 63 percent of those polled, connected 'Here's Johnny' with Carson or his show."

(All Mailer did was suggest to Wallace and the television audience that President Dwight D. Eisenhower was "a bit of a woman.") We can see today that the real charm of television, what keeps us coming back to it and its most successful performers and shows, is the gentleness of its ritual. As we enter the nineties, perhaps that is changing. We now have a whole slew of mean-spirited televised nonfiction. But will those shows last? Will they last the thirty years Carson has lasted?

Like that of many of the comedians he reveres, Carson's own humor has been anything but cutting-edge. Its dominant quality has been gentleness. Even in satire, the Nebraska boy is both gentle and mannerly. In that, his humor has been Middle American, perhaps an almost artistic display of everything that Middle America has produced in the way of human character.

Take, for instance, his satiric impersonations of former president Ronald Reagan. Here lie both the wit and charm of his style. Allow Abbott and Costello doing "Who's on First?" to rattle around in your brain a bit. Then see Carson made up to look more like President Reagan than President Reagan. Remember that Reagan's embattled secretary of the interior at the time was James Watt. We see Reagan sitting in the Oval Office. His secretary of state comes through the door and takes the chair next to the desk.

*"Morning, Mr. President . . . Mr. President, your press conference is scheduled to begin in an hour, so there's not much time for me to brief you on the kind of subjects that the press may throw at you."*

*"I know the environment is on their minds, and I'm sure they'll ask me about my secretary of the interior."*

*"What?"*

*"Jim, I just told you. I think they'll ask about my secretary of the interior."*

*"His name is Watt. You're scheduled to go swimming with him tomorrow morning at the Y."*

*"Where?"*

*"Y."*

*"Why?"*

*"That's right. With Watt.*

*"With what? I don't even know with who?"*

*"Not 'who.' Watt."*

*"Where?"*

*"Y."*

*"Let's go on to the Middle East now. I'll need the first name of the head of the PLO. That . . . ah . . . Arafat guy."*

*"Yasir."*

*"I said, I'll need the first name of the head of the PLO."*

*"Yasir."*

*"Jim, it's nice of you to be polite, but . . ."*

The routine is, of course, just another way of doing "Who's on First?" Don't feel sorry for Abbott and Costello; they borrowed it from a vaudeville routine called "The Baker's Dozen." Both uses are consistent with an older view of comedy, that the timeless routines of vaudeville belong to a common stock, that the quality of the material is determined by its delivery, by that all-important element—timing. It is not a humor that ever promises to make its audience uncomfortable, to make its audience squirm. Leave that for Eddie Murphy or Louie Anderson when they are brought on. It isn't Carson's style.

Mr. Rambo's Neighborhood? Now that is classic Carson style. Mr. Reagan's Neighborhood? (There are more than a few similarities in the way Carson conducts his late evening Chautauqua and the way Fred Rogers conducts his early afternoon Chautauqua, come to think of it.) Carson as a post office employee. ("We make sure your letter sees as much of the United States as possible.") Carson as Tarzan in a sketch absolutely brimming with innuendo (or, repressed sexuality, however you want to look at it) playing opposite Betty White. His precisely delivered one-liners. "Over the years, I've seen 'em come and go, and that's just in my house." "Through the years, I've learned to lean on Ed, and Ed has learned to lean on everything." Ed absentmindedly (in front of 20 million viewers) picking a piece of lint off Carson's collar.

Then, of course, there was the night in 1965 when Carson was visited by Groucho Marx. (It was Groucho who introduced Carson to the world on his first night of *The Tonight Show*.) A nurse named Carol Ann had been interviewed first and was sitting to

One night, Angie Dickinson, longtime Tonight guest, came on wearing a red, billowy outfit that caught Johnny's attention. He asked why she was wearing jammies, and then inquired, "Okay, do you dress for men or for women?"

Dickinson stunned Johnny, replying, "Well, I dress for women and I undress for men."

Groucho's right. Carson had the comic sense to stay out of their banter until precisely the right moment, looking almost sheepishly into the camera all the while and pretending to read a piece of paper he had in his hand.

GROUCHO (to the young lady on his right): *How are you? In addition to that, who are you? That's even more important.*

CAROL ANN:     *Carol Ann.*

GROUCHO:       *What are you, two girls?*

CARSON:        *Say the secret word and Groucho will come to your house.*

GROUCHO:       *I see, my dressing room isn't good enough for her!*

CAROL ANN:     *My patients are in the hospital. I don't make house calls.*

GROUCHO:       *Are you a physician?*

CAROL ANN:     *No. Registered nurse.*

GROUCHO:       *Oh really. Where are you registered? Any place where I can see you?*

We have all been able to see Mr. Carson nearly every weeknight for three decades. There has never been any question where he was registered. *The Tonight Show* without him, no matter how greatly conceived, will not be *The Tonight Show* we have known. Distilled from nearly a century of show business, *The Tonight Show Starring Johnny Carson* exhibited our present and ourselves in a manner that will not likely be replicated. Don't grieve. That, too, befits a society that has always placed its greatest value in the new, even while longing for the old.

One fears the new—not necessarily the new *Tonight Show,* for it seems to have been left in good hands; but the new mirror television will hold up to our face may be harsher and perhaps a good deal more exotic. *Candid Camera* has made a comeback as this is written, and home videos of the most excruciating sort have also been turned into prime-time entertainment. Perhaps such ugliness will fade quickly, and others of the Carson sort will emerge from the plains of Nebraska. Perhaps.

But there will not be another ritual like *The Tonight Show*, the ritual of Carson the insomniac, the ever-evolving every-night touchstone of American popular culture.

*AUTHOR'S NOTE: John Lofflin, a diagnostic scrutinizer of all he observes (with great precision, I might add), has been a journalist and free-lance writer since 1970. Curiously, he delights in viewing television sans the audio, pleasing his eyes with just the picture, examining, absorbing, and filing mental storage. He teaches media studies and journalism at Park College in Parkville, Missouri. He has written for* Money magazine, The New York Times, *and many Midwest newspapers. Currently, he writes a weekly column for an alternative newspaper in Kansas City,* The Pitch, *and is coauthor of* The Official Abbott & Costello Scrapbook *(Contemporary Books, 1990). Over the years, he's enjoyed the many jazz and blues artists Johnny has welcomed on the show—with the volume on.*

# "More to Come"

More than just the bright feathers of the NBC peacock have fluttered out the doors of the network graphic-arts department.

Some of that department's most talked-about artwork are the objets d'art sandwiched between commercial breaks of *The Tonight Show*. Sometimes called "bumpers" or "art cards," and commonly known as "More to Comes" around the office, this elite artistic expression, shown nightly on network television, probably generates as much success for the artist as a shot on the air would provide a comic.

The pieces are memorable, but, naturally, not as identifiable as the Mona Lisa. Then again, the Mona

One of the first art cards used on *The Tonight Show* produced in the 1960s by Art Trugman. *(courtesy of Art Trugman)*

NBC artist Art Trugman body-painted for cast members on TV's *Laugh-In* in the 1960s. *(courtesy of Art Trugman)*

Lisa is stuck in the Louvre and doesn't enjoy nightly exposure to millions of Americans. For the long line of television artists, *The Tonight Show* is the Louvre or the Metropolitan Museum of Art. And the Mona Lisa never won an Emmy. Simply because the medium exposes work to the masses in numbers beyond the expectations of anyone who ever stretched a canvas, the appreciation and value of the artwork displayed on the screen should not be diminished.

Originally, says Art Trugman, a thirty-nine-year NBC employee, the "More to Comes" developed into themes. When Carson took over *The Tonight Show* in New York, Trugman was a young artist in the graphics department and made the move to Los Angeles with the rest of the *Tonight Show* crew. His real claim to fame had been body painting. Remember the bikini-clad beauties on TV's *Laugh-In*? It was Trugman, brush in hand, who happily painted words, shapes, faces, and golf balls around the navels of Goldie Hawn, Judy Carne, and other 1960s shapely women who shimmied gently for the oddball comics Rowan and Martin in their hit variety show

Today, Trugman heads the NBC graphic-arts de-

**Art Trugman, head of NBC's graphic-arts department, produced some of the earliest "More to Come" placards for the show.** *(courtesy of NBC Graphics)*

partment, protecting, encouraging, and developing the talents of his young staff like a proud father. Besides creating artwork for *The Tonight Show*, the staff artists conceptualize logos for television shows, create signs, cereal boxes, props, and posters for every use in television. Their work is even seen on other major networks. Their reputation is the best.

"When I first came here, it was myself and Dave Rose," Trugman remembers. "We drew little sight gags for the 'More to Comes,' like the two Eskimos rubbing noses." Another early slide had Tarzan hanging on a vine over an alligator with the words "Hang in There" printed alongside. Eventually, the themes within the show illustrated animals, performers, musicians, comedians, zodiac signs, and an array of unusual expressions. Each artist called on to contribute a set—consisting of ten different pieces when the show ran an hour and a half, and now usually six slides—put his or her heart and soul into their "babies," says Trugman. With nearly ten artists employed in the department at any given time, these creations are the network's prized pieces. They are the pièce de résistance of the television art world. They can mean a stepping-stone for young artists. "A lot of kids have busted away and done very well," says Trugman.

Accolades are rare in the art department; however, staff artisans Rick Andreoli and Susan Cuscuna picked up Emmy Award nominations for their "More to Come" conceptions in the 1974–75 race. The category was listed as "Outstanding Achievement in Graphic Design and Title Sequences for a Single Episode of a Series or for a Special Program."

These famous visuals, usually sixteen by twenty inches or eighteen by twenty-four inches, are created in whatever method the artist prefers. They cannot be too involved or too intricate lest they not "read" on television when flashed for the viewer. After completion by the artist, they are shot into slides and handed to the technical personnel who incorporate them into the show by shooting them on tape. And from there, America enjoys a few nightly nine-second studies in art, compliments of NBC.

"This is the best part of the job for me," says artist Don Locke, who started with NBC in 1980. "It's given me the opportunity to experiment with all kinds of styles. I work in markers, acrylics, airbrush, pencils."

His favorite set is the jazz performers he created in markers on a chemically treated photographic paper, which appear like bleeding watercolors. His first set, still seen occasionally, features comedy stars like Harold Lloyd hanging from the hands of an oversized clock face, W. C. Fields, and the Marx Brothers. He's produced a series on sports figures, dancers, "and always tries something new," says his boss, Trugman, who might be his biggest fan.

Only once did the graphics department stray from its own stable of artisans for a "More to Come" image. "We hired a lady who was very unique in making little clay figures about three inches tall,"

**Artist Don Locke preparing "More to Come" artwork in 1991.** *(courtesy of Don Locke)*

Trugman says. "She did a whole set of an old couple watching television in bed, in a sauna, from their couch. It was real cute." Rarely does Trugman accept submissions in the mail, but he's considered suggestions supplied by fans of the show. Artists across the country have aspired to create a *Tonight Show* set, "but we have to stick with the artists on staff and give them a chance," Trugman explains with a hint of regret. "Freelance artists call me constantly. The kids here come first."

Johnny Carson, who has always remained proud of the art, enjoys peeking at the new sets on the monitor when they are premiered on the show. He has never requested one to hang in his office, or suppressed the staff's creative expressions, but he's complimented some that catch his eye. "He never comes into our office," Trugman says. "He can be a bit of a cold fish sometimes. He did come in here recently to get his passport picture taken."

**Andrew Hoyos, Art Trugman, and Michael Bayouth display their creations that aired on *The Tonight Show* in the 1970s.**

This silence, at best, might be described as a blessing for the artists who wish to express their images and experiment in varying techniques. Each is professional in his own way; the individuals are not starving artists peddling their wares on the street corner where a gas station has been boarded up. No felt paint-by-number Elvis portraits here. Some of the *Tonight Show* gems are worthy of placement in museums, many artists attest, and they range from abstract visuals to realism that provides a wonderful parade for audiences.

Former staff artist Rick Andreoli produced a set on women. They were anything but normal. "He was a bachelor, you know, and the women were in different positions," says Trugman. "One woman was on all fours, behind bars like a lion in a cage. She had long hair like a mane. We had to take it off because there were complaints, but there was nothing vulgar about it. Some pieces we have to watch because they might be too complicated and they won't 'read' quick enough on the air."

The NBC legal department was summoned twice for creations that aired on *The Tonight Show*. One, a realistic conception of a photograph of Albert Einstein, prompted a remuneration request from the estate of the late photographer who shot the wiry-haired genius in the 1940s. Another instance is a cartoon carousel horse painted by Don Locke that utilized the image Locke found in a photograph as a model. Although Locke's rendition was clearly not a direct copy, NBC paid twenty-five hundred dollars as a nuisance fee to the photographer; if it had progressed to litigation, however, NBC would probably have prevailed.

There is no limit to the themes displayed on *Tonight* via these canvas crafts. Cowboys, childstars, lions, cartoon clocks, boiling teakettles and ringing telephones, classic actors, horror monsters, and singers all flash by while Doc's orchestra blasts through the screen. Two per night say *The Tonight Show Starring Johnny Carson*, with the rest labeled "More to Come." And when a show is repeated, those who select "More to Comes" are careful not to include zodiac bumpers of the inappropriate month. The stars were not in line one night when a mishap occurred and the network was deluged with letters from angry astrologers.

Many collectors have inquired about obtaining the original pieces, and to date NBC has released a few for public auction. A few have trickled out possibly "leaked" by their creators. No doubt after Johnny's retirement, these little masterpieces will fetch top dollar at auction if NBC decides to disburse the art.

"Two to three publishers have approached us about doing a "More to Come" art coffee-table book," says Trugman of the proposed project. "A private company which called itself the More to Come Company made a deal with Carson Productions some years ago to produce a massive merchandising line on the art. T-shirts, posters, books, placemats. For a year, they were collecting items and organizing, but it fell through."

**Johnny Carson amid some of the most popular art ever presented on television.** *(courtesy of NBC)*

# 10

## Who They Really Are

### Johnny

The most demystifying part of attending a taping in Studio One in Burbank and actually exploring the set with one's own eyes is the actual size of it all—an astonishment every newcomer experiences. It's sort of a culture shock. The whole stage seems so marvelously ostentatious on television. How long it seems to take Johnny to stroll over to Doc at the bandstand. The stage where Johnny's desk seems to be a fair-sized step up from the floor. The proscenium behind Johnny's couch seems deep, distant, and dreamy.

None of it is true. The distance between Johnny and Doc is a mere ten yards. Johnny only takes about nine steps from the curtain to his spot for the monologue. The midnight skyline of Los Angeles behind him is a mere few feet from his perch. The stage is scarcely six inches off the ground. The whole aura of grand-scale television has fooled the viewers for years, all created by the three television cameras stationed between the audience and the set.

The desk, the couch, the small set is the "home" that Johnny has spent countless hours entertaining his guests in. He's most comfortable behind his desk, he says, once dragging along a collapsible brown replica to sit behind on *Late Night with David Letterman*, as the guest that night. *Tonight Show* guest George Peppard convinced Johnny to trade places one night and let *him* sit at the desk for a while. Immediately uncomfortable, Carson ad-libbed his way back to the throne.

It's a familiar sight that everyone can just about envision with accurate detail: the layout of the studio, the items on Johnny's desk, the couch where Ed sits and hovers over guests (and, I guess, lies down for a snooze, out of sight, as more guests arrive). Not only has the *Tonight Show* agenda remained the same (and, some say, the guest list), just about everything in the "house" has been a constant. Its surroundings are friendly, warm, and inviting.

The broadcasts that emanated from New York's Studio 6B exposed a tiny set, dull in detail, and decorated very modestly. The lighting was not elaborate, or as strategically intimate as today's visual effects.

The sixties furnishings were tiny in frame, low-key in fluff, and limited in comfort for lounging. Although shown in black-and-white, it was probably that bright orange vinyl upholstery that you still see in your aunt's living room, the one that hasn't been redecorated in twenty-five years. Remember? Johnny's television living room was not much different than what you might find in any home at that time. The desk was simple

An animated moment during Johnny's monologue in 1967. *(from the author's collection)*

Johnny Carson has remained a national habit for so long, so intensely, and so intimately, one reporter noted "that his final year of *Tonight* is turning into the sentimental equivalent of a beloved diva's farewell tour." *(from the author's collection)*

like a box; the background consisted of block designs attached to the wall, or vertical panels, sort of streaks in a mod design, yet not too distracting.

When color television was popularized beginning in the midsixties, the carpeting on the show was changed, the set was jazzed up, and even makeup on the performers had to be altered a bit. The wavy neapolitan curtain Johnny greeted his crowds from has always been an impressive sight on crisp, clear color television, no matter how accustomed audiences were to its pattern. (After Carson announced his retirement, one audience member suggested on the show that he have the famous curtain cut in squares and auctioned for charity. Not a bad idea.)

Still, the layout of the room never changed over three decades. Johnny sat at his desk, and the guests in the hot seat peered over their left shoulder to chat with him. Later on, a little motorized footstool was installed that would slide out from beneath the seat when the host flipped a switch behind the desk; this was an exclusive luxury for those diminutive-sized guests who entered the domain. His aim was to make his guests comfortable, it seemed, although at least one who stopped by disagreed.

Former *Tomorrow* show host Tom Snyder told *TV Guide* about his first impression of meeting Carson face-to-face on the air: "You are sitting in this awful chair," he said. "I mean a chair that has got to be the most uncomfortable chair in the history of television. At the break, I say, 'Johnny, is this chair uncomfortable on purpose?' He says, 'Yep. That's right. I need all the weapons I can get to keep people off their guard.'"

Carl Reiner, who has sat next to Carson dozens of times, says it's not like home, but rather an office. "You feel like you're in an office being interviewed," he says, describing the set. "But if you know you have the qualifications for the job, you don't feel so bad.

"I like the house that Johnny's built. There are new houses like Arsenio's—a couple of couches," Reiner says. "We're just not used to it."

Guest host Dick Shawn turned the desk and the chairs over on their sides one night in a final effort to force laughs from the audience when his material failed. (This infuriated Carson.) Shawn was not invited to repeat his guest-hosting chores.

And on occasion, the prop department had brought in balsa-wood replicas it called "breakaway desks" for stunts and gags. Carnac stumbled right on top of it, demolishing the piece of furniture. A samurai warrior has chopped one to bits. Steve Martin blew the prop up one night, with "dynamite." Johnny had a fruitcake forklifted in one holiday, placed the thirty-pound cake on the top of his desk, and watched it crash clear through—damage one might imagine the clichéd cake could do.

Johnny joked that when he leaves, he's taking the desk with him. In fact, the entire Studio One, which features permanent theater seating, was rarely used for any other show or performer other than Johnny. Many Bob Hope specials have been taped there, but Hope's had clout at NBC.

To the host, the desk is sacred, like the items that rest upon it. Usually adorning the surface are several items: a microphone, coffee mug, cigarette lighter, wooden cigarette box, two-headed pencils, and papers. The desk, if you'll recall, has taken its beatings over the years. Animals have urinated and let the wants of nature plop all over it. It's felt the scald of spilled coffee, the chill of cold water, Johnny's sticky apple juice, champagne, and stronger brews.

Untouched for years, the simple brown cigarette box that always sat on the edge of the desk was broken one night when Johnny was gone. When he returned, he abruptly noticed—on-camera—that the cherished memento that he had brought from New York had been tampered with. Beaten. The lid was in pieces.

Don Rickles was the culprit, he was told by the audience and Doc Severinsen, who was sitting in for Ed.

In a sketch about NBC's miniseries *Shogun*, a samurai hacks apart Johnny's desk in 1980. *(Wide World Photo)*

"He was having one of his fits," Doc told Johnny.

"How could you tell?" Johnny asked.

Infuriated, Carson suddenly got up from his seat, grabbed a hand mike, and waved a cameraman to follow him across the hallway into the next studio where Rickles was taping his sitcom *CPO Sharkey* in front of a live audience. Carson burst into the studio, halted the taping, and lashed a verbal beating to the man who delivers them best. Rickles was stunned and then apologetic, attempting to cover his embarrassment with humor, as usual. With a tinge of humor, Carson joked at the situation, but was visibly angered by the whole affair.

Johnny and Ed have had fun with the set. Like a childhood home, it was familiar, usually cozy, and always there. Occasionally, the scene behind Johnny changed from a lakeside view to a high-rise-building panorama to a wintery snow scene. Since arriving in Los Angeles, seven alterations have been made in the proscenium, not counting the cross grids added to provide an appearance of a window.

Props such as a snow machine have been hung above the set, just behind Johnny, allowing white fluff to fall at the flick of a switch. At Christmas, Johnny turned the snow on, delighted like a little boy with a new toy. One night Johnny decided to turn on the prop fog machine (commenting on the excessive smog in Los Angeles), and the switch malfunctioned. Johnny and Ed couldn't stop coughing and laughing at the obvious foul-up. The stage quickly became flooded with fog before it shut itself off. "When we have a special effect," joked Carson, "we go all the way."

Delivering the monologue one nice June evening, Johnny stopped and turned his head toward his desk. He couldn't take his eyes off abrupt new carpeting, recently laid around the set. It was a pattern of large, bright red-and-black swirls—something you might see on a subway wall, i.e., loud graffiti. Nonchalant and pleasant for television, it wasn't. And yet, it had been installed to the specifications of everyone on the show; they hadn't realized its impact until it was installed and unveiled on camera. Johnny joked about the carpeting, and the audience heartily agreed.

Next night, Johnny came out with a bulky necktie made of the same gaudy pattern as the carpet. When the lights came up on the set, his whole desk had been wrapped in the colorful rug. Carpet-layers were brought in for another job quickly thereafter.

## The Mighty Carson

VITALS:

BIRTHPLACE: Corning, Iowa (although he grew up in Norfolk, Nebraska)
BIRTHDATE: October 23, 1925
HEIGHT: 5'11"
WEIGHT: 170 lbs., average
HAIR: gray/white
EYES: hazel
MARRIED: four times; children are three boys: Chris, Ricky, and Cory
CURRENT RESIDENCE: Malibu, California

When he walked out that opening night, October 1, 1962, he looked at the beaming audience and said, "I want my na-na." He knew he had some big shoes to fill on *The Tonight Show.* Thirty years later, the man is such an institution on television —a real late-night friend to millions of Americans, most of whom have never seen him in person— Johnny Carson can't even leave his home for fear of a mob scene. *The Tonight Show,* pointed out *Look* magazine even in 1979, "has become an institution as familiar and comfortable as Coca-Cola and

McDonald's. . . ." And its longtime charming host has become an icon. He joked on the air once of this notion: "I was in the grocery store, and this lady approached me and said, 'My God, Johnny Carson! What are you doing here?'

"'I'm hungry,'" I told her, "'so I'm shopping.'"

The scenario is a familiar one for one Johnny Carson, maybe the most recognized man in America. His identity is living proof of the clichéd "household word" in motion, and rarely can he emerge from his residence for a quiet mo-

Unscheduled guest Groucho Marx introduced Johnny Carson to America as the new host of *The Tonight Show* on October 1, 1962. *(Personality Photos, Inc.)*

He's been called "the ideal American personality," topped by maybe only Will Rogers in such overwhelming appeal and popularity.

ment in public. What a life that must be. Half the people who approach him want his autograph. The other half want to audition their spoon-playing act right there at the restaurant table for him, fame glittering in their eyes.

He's been asked for autographs while standing at the urinal, and people have even followed him home from work as he drives the course from NBC to Malibu each day.

Walter Kempley, one of his former writers, put it into perspective: "Johnny feels a terrible burden when he appears in public," Kempley explained when Carson lived in New York. "He wanted to take his sons to the Bronx Zoo but felt his presence would cause too much of an uproar for his sons to enjoy the trip. One night I walked into his dressing room, and he was sitting there with a mustache and a full beard pasted on his face. He looked like one of the Smith Brothers. The makeup man had fixed it up for him so he could make the zoo trip. Johnny fitted on a wig and told me to walk with him in the hallway to see if his disguise would work. . . . We met three people in the hall. Strangers. Every single one said, 'Hi Johnny,' and he turned around and shuffled back to his dressing room."

Johnny says he understands the compromise he must make when in the public light, so he is generous with signatures and snapshots for fans. He is, after all, a celebrity, but a private one, if at all possible.

Bel Kaufman thinks he reflects the "great American majority—its values, its myths." The writer put it this way: "He is the American dream personified: the typical middle-aged goy-next-door who has come out of Nebraska and become a self-made millionaire. Everything about him is American: his face, his voice, his background. He speaks of an average boyhood in an average family in an average home. He enjoys tennis, playing the drums, doing magical tricks. He is a good sport, willing to try anything once. . . . He is not afraid to appear ridiculous. He is kind and decent to children and old ladies. He keeps abreast of the news, is mildly liberal, purposely anti-intellectual. At the peak of his career . . . he is energetic, physically fit. That's American. Even his name is an American-boy name: not John, not Jack, but Johnny."

John William Carson was born in Corning, Iowa, on October 23, 1925, to Homer Lloyd and Ruth Hook Carson. He grew up in a large frame house in Norfolk, Nebraska, the territory he really regards as roots.

Believe it or not, young Johnny was a shy child, uncomfortable *in* crowds, but he soon learned to enjoy being *in front* of them. His childhood was secure, his family, which included an older sister, Catherine, and a younger brother, Richard, spent family vacations on a lake in Minnesota. His father was a utility-company lineman who became a manager for the Nebraska Light and Power Company. The family's church was Methodist, and at school Carson's notable Popeye impression

**A young Johnny Carson as "The Great Carsoni," his early magic act in 1949.** *(Personality Photos, Inc.)*

and talent for jokes called attention to him, releasing his shyness and anxiety somewhat.

Early on, maybe age twelve or so, Johnny stumbled across *Hoffmann's Book of Magic* and quickly became engrossed in the art of illusion, enthralled with the whole process of making magic. He sent away for mail-order magic kits, practiced the art of card tricks, and pestered his family with "pick a card . . . c'mon, take a card." At age fourteen, young John appeared "live" at the Norfolk Rotary Club, which earned him three dollars. His mother had sewn him a big black cape he swung on his shoulders, and he became the first Mighty Carson Art Player in his very first routine—as "The Great Carsoni." Eventually, he entertained at parties for his family, encouraged by his parents to proceed with the prestidigitation.

At Norfolk High School, he appeared in student productions, and wrote a humor column for the school newspaper. To earn funds to pay for his magic, he was ushering at the Granada Theater and selling subscriptions to the *Saturday Evening Post*—never knowing he would someday adorn the cover. He graduated in 1943 and entered World War II, was inducted into the navy and sent to midshipmen's school at Columbia University. He served the rest of the war aboard the *USS Pennsylvania* in the Pacific Ocean. Reportedly, he was "the only officer to entertain enlisted men in the ship's shows."

He earned a B.A. degree at the University of Nebraska, while he was pledged to Phi Gamma Delta. His senior thesis, entitled "Comedy Writing," was a study in the art via an analysis of radio comics like Jack Benny, Bob Hope, and Fred Allen—all of whom he later worked with in amazement and awe. Just prior to his graduation in 1949, he obtained his first professional radio job at KRAB in Lincoln, Nebraska. Later, he found

Ensign Johnny Carson served in the navy during World War II. *(courtesy of NBC)*

One of Johnny's guests was an actor who told of his bad luck with women. He told Johnny he had invited a girl over for dinner and she stayed for three months. Then the guest added, "But she was a good cook." Johnny replied, "Three months! She must have made good bed . . . bread!"

JACK BENNY: For years and years I've been Johnny Carson's idol. . . . Then all of a sudden, the whole thing switched, and Johnny Carson became my idol. And do you want to know something? It's not *nearly* as much fun this way! *(courtesy of the author's collection)*

work at WOW radio in Omaha, before moving to California, where he became an "all-purpose" announcer at KNXT-TV (now KCBS) in Los Angeles and was given his own half-hour comedy show on Sunday afternoons, *Carson's Cellar*. The young black-haired comic hosted the show until mid-1953. The show caught the attention of Groucho Marx, Fred Allen, and Red Skelton, all of whom graced the tiny television studio to appear with the rookie on this new thing called television. They were testing the medium at the same time as young John Carson. Carson's first big TV appearance on an established show was with Jack Benny in 1952. He mimicked Benny's stance and stare, and comically offered suggestions to the master as to "how to do Benny." He told Benny he spoke too slowly and to try not to put his hand up to his face so much. Benny quizzed, "How long have you been in show business?" The routine went extremely well, and the two comedians—one a living legend, the other a protégé—became close friends from then on. (Carson guest-starred on many of Benny's later TV specials, and in return, Benny stopped by the *Tonight Show* for some wonderful, memorable interviews that remain in Johnny's all-time-favorite category.)

Recalling this comic named Carson, comedian Red Skelton hired him as a writer on his CBS-TV show. In August 1954, fate turned Johnny's way when a breakaway door malfunctioned during rehearsal just two hours

before airtime, and Skelton was knocked unconscious. The producer hastily asked Carson to go on in lieu of Skelton, and with a nearly impromptu monologue he'd thought of while driving to the studio, he impressed the audiences. He also impressed CBS executives who handed him his own program, *The Johnny Carson Show*, which lasted just thirty-nine weeks on the air. It was a rocky start, and the show went through seven writers and eight directors. Johnny's failure at the show prompted his only

Johnny is the court jester in a sketch with the monumental actor Orson Welles in 1976. *(Personality Photos, Inc.)*

The new host of *Do You Trust Your Wife?* which was later renamed *Who Do You Trust?* (1957). *(Personality Photos, Inc.)*

Always suffering through formal photography sessions, Johnny Carson complained to *TV Guide* once, "Why can't you folks come over to the show and shoot while we're taping? You can't get any decent pictures standing somebody up against a backdrop and saying 'Smile!' Smile at what?" Maybe his paycheck? *(Personality Photos, Inc.)*

Publicity for *The Tonight Show* in the Big Apple. *(courtesy of Steve Randisi)*

recourse, a removal to New York. On borrowed money, he shifted coasts in 1956. He joined the Friars Club and made guest appearances on different TV shows; after his reputation in the comedy world had been rebuilt from the *Johnny Carson Show* blow, his self-confidence was restored. He hosted the network show, *Earn Your Vacation*, at age twenty-nine, while also appearing as a substitute host for another upcoming TV personality, Jack Paar, on CBS's *The Morning Show*. In

1957, he was hired as host of ABC-TV's quiz game show *Who Do You Trust?* which lasted five years with Carson as the master of ceremonies, and his new associate, Ed McMahon, served as announcer. While host, Johnny had been offered the position as new *Tonight Show* host in 1958 prior to Jack Paar, but declined, based on his security with his current program. Then, in 1962, NBC boosted its financial offer and lured Carson to *Tonight*. To say he is surprised he stayed with the show for three decades would be entirely accurate.

During the *Tonight Show* stretch, Carson's interest in differing endeavors included his own apparel company and production company, *Carson Productions*. He headlined in Las Vegas regularly at the Sahara Hotel, and also appeared at Resorts International in Atlantic City, New Jersey. Personally, Carson has always remained (some say almost forcibly because of his fame) a homebody. He enjoys tennis, the drums, and astronomy, and

One of Johnny Carson's passions is to play the drums, which relieves hostility, he says. *(Personality Photos, Inc.)*

Johnny joking with his brother, Dick Carson, who directed *The Tonight Show* in 1967. *(Personality Photos, Inc.)*

is an avid reader on many topics.

Carson is the recipient of a plethora of awards and accolades such as Harvard University's Hasty Pudding Man of the Year Award, Entertainer of the Year Award from the American Guild of Variety Artists, and the Friars Club Man of the Year award in 1965 and in 1979. Just about every major magazine has featured profiles on him (*The New Yorker, Rolling Stone*, the *Saturday Evening Post, TV Guide, Time, Look, Life, People, Us*).

## Married Life

*JOHNNY CARSON [after explaining that an old lady stopped him on the street]: "She says, 'Johnny, I want a divorce from you.' And I said, 'But we're not even married.' She says, 'Yeah, but I want to skip right to the goodies.'"*

To say his married life has been tumultuous is to let the man off easy. Carson has admitted that his devotion to his career has made his marriages suffer. Although he's not been down the aisle as frequently as Elizabeth Taylor or Mickey Rooney, the news has not been any less powerful along the tabloid trail.

Reprinted with permission from *TV Guide* magazine. © 1955 by News America Publications, Inc., Radnor, Pennsylvania.

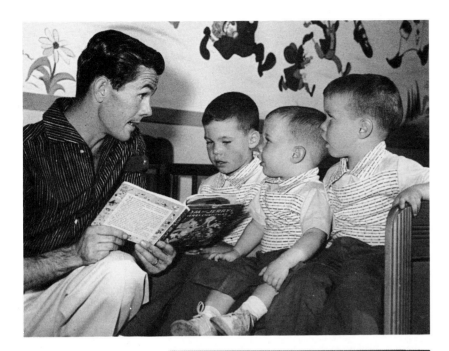

Johnny reads a tale before bedtime to his three kids, Kit, Cory, and Ricky, in 1955. *(courtesy of CBS)*

His first marriage, to college sweetheart Jody Wolcott, took place in Nebraska in 1949. The couple had three boys, Chris, Ricky, and Cory. In 1963, they obtained a "quickie" Mexican divorce.

Airline stewardess Joanne Copeland was his second wife. They joined in matrimony in 1963, right after his *Tonight Show* duties began. During this marriage, Johnny was a workaholic. He won the ratings of his fans, but not in his marriage. Joanne left after seven years. Their divorce, splashed across every tabloid imaginable, was made final in 1972.

Johnny and Joanne (née Copeland) share champagne at a small reception in the Carson apartment after their marriage on August 17, 1963, at New York's Marble Collegiate Church on Fifth Avenue. Johnny was thirty-seven and Joanne was thirty-one. *(Personality Photos, Inc.)*

Johnny and Joanna, his third wife, share a warm moment for the photographer at rehearsals for the twenty-ninth annual SHARE presentation, a charity benefit for the mentally retarded in 1982. *(Wide World Photo)*

An irate Johnny Carson angrily read from a copy of the *National Enquirer* and denounced an article about troubles within his marriage as "scurrilous" and said the publication "stinks." He concluded, "I'm going to call the *National Enquirer* and the people who wrote this liars. Now that's slander. They can sue me for slander. You know where I am, gentlemen. . . . I'll be happy to defend that charge against you." *(Wide World Photo)*

James Albert, author of *Pay Dirt,* noted: "While Johnny publicly accepted the blame for not spending as much time on their relationship as he did on his new show, his sentiments weren't sweet enough for Joanne. After a protracted divorce, she took him for nearly half a million dollars in cash and art and $100,000 a year in alimony for life. Interestingly, after the divorce, she went back to college and earned a Ph.D. in nutrition. Then she hosted cable TV's *Alive and Well Show.*"

At *The Tonight Show*'s tenth anniversary party on September 30, 1972, Johnny announced that he and former model Joanna Holland had been secretly married that afternoon, shocking all of his friends and associates at the party. Carson was forty-six, Joanna was thirty-three, and the two moved into a luxurious $5 million Bel Air mansion that once belonged to movie producer Mervyn LeRoy. Within a few years, Johnny's pay had escalated to epic proportions while NBC agreed to shorten his *Tonight Show* program from ninety minutes to an hour, and reduced his workweek to four (in some weeks three) nights a week. He was receiving fifteen weeks' vacation as well, all to keep the show fresh and retain his sanity on the show. Otherwise, he would become bored with the show, he explained.

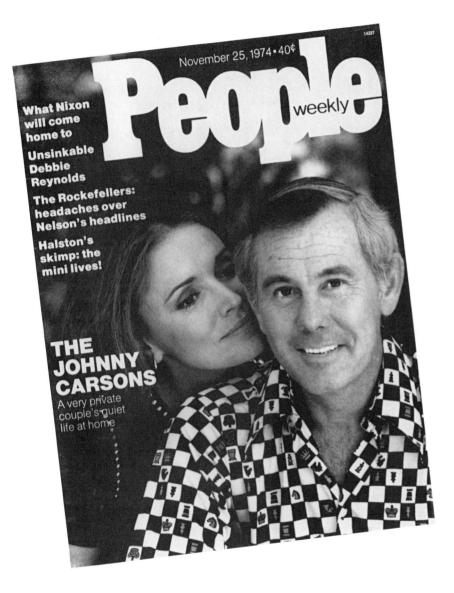

November 25, 1974 • 40¢

# People weekly

14227

What Nixon will come home to

Unsinkable Debbie Reynolds

The Rockefellers: headaches over Nelson's headlines

Halston's skimp: the mini lives!

THE JOHNNY CARSONS
A very private couple's quiet life at home

On March 8, 1983, Joanna filed for divorce at the Clerk of Court's Office at the Los Angeles County Courthouse. Over the next two years, a battle ensued that would set many ignominious records. One writer observed: "Joanna didn't just want to take Johnny to the cleaners, she wanted to leave him hanging on the clothesline out back." Johnny joked on the show, "My producer, Freddy de Cordova, really gave me something I needed for Christmas. He gave me a gift certificate to the legal office of Jacoby and Meyers."

Johnny and his fourth wife,
the former Alex Mass.
*(Wide World Photo)*

In 1983, Joanna filed an application asking the judge to order Johnny to pay her $220,000 per month in temporary alimony, "in order that I can maintain my standard of living which I have enjoyed during the past several years." Additional funds were sought: $500,000 in attorney fees, and $176,000 to begin the work of stripping Johnny's books. She claimed $220,000 a month in expenses, and wanted Johnny to foot the complete bill.

Johnny joked in the monologue again: "Passed by my house yesterday—in a tour bus."

She claimed she needed funds to support others, her grown son from another marriage, limousine services, and $270 a month to care for her cat, which Johnny insisted was not there when they were married. In household expenses, Joanna wanted fourteen hundred dollars monthly for food money. Johnny balked all the way. He claimed there was no way she could eat that much in groceries in a month. Her claims for funds were lengthy, and Johnny's attorneys explained to the judge that Joanna's claims were "wildly exaggerated."

In an oblique comment on his show, Johnny said, "I heard from my cat's lawyer. . . . My cat wants twelve thousand dollars a week for Tender Vittles."

Author James Albert writes: "As Judge Olson and the attorneys argued over the details, Johnny braced himself. He knew full well that under California's community property laws, Joanna was entitled to 50% of all the assets accumulated during the marriage even though he was the one who worked and earned virtually 100% of the couple's income during that time. . . . What emerged on August 30, 1985, was an 80-page divorce settlement to which Johnny and Joanna agreed." Albert pointed out that the whopping, meticulous document was more detailed and much longer than the World War I Armistice with Germany, the World War II Japanese and Germany Instruments of Surrender, the 1782 treaty between England and the American colonies ending the Revolutionary War, the Louisiana Purchase, the Treaty of Ghent ending the War of 1812 and the United Nations Charter . . . combined.

After three divorces have ravaged his earnings, angered him by their public display, and left him still wealthy—yet skeptical about remarriage, Johnny married Alex Maas on June 20, 1987. He was sixty-one, she was thirty-five. It wasn't until nine days later that the press was informed of the marriage. They reside in Malibu, California, next to the beach, where Johnny first saw Alex walking . . . and was intrigued by the beautiful woman he saw.

## Through Thick and Thick

Possibly the only constant element in the adult life of Johnny Carson has been his pal Ed McMahon. His life has been good, but not without trouble. Earning his success at NBC, he seemed to bear the whole, necessary package: charisma, age and energy, the yearning, the talent, appeal, opportunity, and expertise. To the public, he may have lived a fairy-tale existence throughout the *Tonight Show* years, but remember, this Carson fellow is not superhuman. Some might speculate that with the amount of wealth and fame he attained, the chances of anything going awry in his life are slim. Maybe you'd like to trade lives if you could? Johnny Carson might suggest that intelligent people would wisely avoid that contemplation altogether. His life has not been utopian. He has three failed marriages and other family concerns, like most Americans. So let's contribute one more "apple pie" conclusion: No one's perfect. That's definitely American.

Although Carson has always strived to keep his personal life out of the public eye there was one instance, shortly after his announcement about leaving NBC, where he openly and poignantly discussed one of his family members.

With audience members wiping tears from their eyes, and Johnny holding them back, the host's voice choked with emotion as he delivered a brief tribute to his son who had died in a freak automobile accident.

When he returned from a hiatus on July 17, 1991, audiences were wondering if he might mention the death of his son Rick, a thirty-nine-year-old photographer, who died just days prior when his Nissan Pathfinder rolled down a ravine in Cayucos, California.

Johnny was greeted with wild, supportive applause from the packed Studio One audience. He joked as usual, which attests to his performing abilities. *People* magazine reported: "For perhaps the first time ever, Carson's pain was visible. In a mere month, the 65-year-old host seemed to have aged a decade.

"Then, in the show's final moments, Carson broke with years of deliberate silence about his family to present a touching tribute to his son."

Carson described his second son as "an exuberant young man, fun to be around . . . He tried too darn hard to please," he said, shaking. Carson proudly and nervously closed the show with a nice picture of his son, since the newspapers were running a driver's license shot; then Johnny introduced a series of Rick's landscape photographs.

"For Carson, Rick's eulogy also meant revealing to approximately 12 million viewers a piece of his inner self," *People* commented. This was a rare sentimental view of a Johnny Carson that even his closest friends have not been permitted to touch.

# The Best of Floyd R. Turbo ("Mr. Silent Majority")

He's been described as "the liberal's foe whose effectiveness as a conservative spokesman is impaired only by his inability to read the TelePrompTer faster than an IRS form." The heavily opinionated Turbo, always decked in plaid hunting garb, stands nervously delivering his mouthful of editorial message, all the while shifting his weight like a little boy who can't find the rest room. He's mangled all the topics: gun control, war, women's lib, hunting ("If God didn't want us to hunt, He wouldn't have given us plaid shirts; I only kill in self-defense—what would you do if a rabbit pulled a knife on you?") He's the Emily Litella of weeknight television ("Never mind!") with a familiar strain of pseudonewscaster Ted Baxter delivering a homemade editorial. His sentences are riddled with syntax errors. Mr. Malaprop himself.

Turbo has been compared to Archie Bunker on many occasions. Johnny Carson, a professed fan of Norman Lear's TV classic *All in the Family*, might possibly have fashioned the blowhard Turbo after witnessing Bunker's televised opposition to gun-control.

The topic of one 1972 *All in the Family* episode ("Archie and the Editorial") had Archie delivering an editorial comment on local television, provoked by a gun-control editorial he saw on television. According to Bunker, guns don't kill—people do. A popular thought. And in Bunker's wisdom, how do you stop people from killing people? "Bring back the death penalty!"

In his twisted rationale, Archie Bunker nervously offered his opinions, which actually reinforce the gun-control issue: "Now I wanna talk about another thing that's on everybody's mind . . . and that's the stickups and your skyjackers here . . . which if it was up to me, I could end the skyjackers tomorrow. All ya gotta do is arm all your passengers. . . ." Later in the day, Archie and family adjourned to Kelsey's Bar, where a man who had seen him on television asked to shake his hand—and then held him up at gunpoint.

Ten years later, Carson told *TV Guide*: "Turbo . . . takes the redneck view of something. What you're doing is showing the stupidity of that particular view so that you can make your point comedically. If he's for handguns and wants everybody to arm themselves, it's obvious to anybody who's watching, the point we're trying to make," he says.

Of Turbo, Carson told *Rolling Stone* reporter Timothy White: ". . . he's the epitome of the redneck ignoramus. I find things each week when I go out to do it that I throw in: his gestures at the wrong time, his not knowing where he's supposed to be, his feeble attempts at humor, his talks about things he doesn't quite understand."

And now . . . a taste of Turbo . . .

## Turbo on Nuclear Reactors

Put me down as one American who favors building nuclear plants. I say nuclear energy plants are safe. Each and every one of us must get into the fight to have DDT. It worked so well that now we don't have to use it anymore because it's working everywhere, in the rivers, in our food, and in our lungs. And what's all this fuss about plutonium: How can something named after a Disney character be dangerous? So what if an atomic plant blows up? The people who say that, they are afraid to die. I'm not afraid to die because all my life I have lived by the good book, the American Legion magazine. They say if there is a leak in a nuclear power plant the radiation can kill you. Nix! Radiation cannot kill you because it contains absolutely no cholesterol. They say atomic radiation can hurt your reproductive organs. My answer is, so can a hockey stick . . . but we don't stop building them. I told my wife that there was a chance that radiation might hurt my reproductive organs, but she said in her opinion it is a small price to pay. Let us assume for the sake of argument that there is an atomic explo-

sion, just for the fun of it. It would have very little bad effect, especially here in Los Angeles where we are shielded by a protective layer of smog.

Sure, nuclear leaks will affect the forest animals. So what if a deer grows up with two rear ends? They're easier to shoot, and that's what America is all about. What do they expect us to use for fuel—buffalo chips? Now, these jerks want to use solar energy for electricity. Doesn't that take the cake? How do they expect me to plug my drill into the sun? I'd need a very big stepladder. . . . Some people are even talking about wind power. Phooey! Who wants windmills on their house? Next thing you know we'll be wearing wooden Dutch shoes and sucking cheese all day. So in my simple way, I'm asking that you support nuclear energy. Remember, being an American means being powerful, proud, and pushy, and in conclusion let me finish by ending. . . . Thank you.

## Turbo on the Draft

Recently this effeminate station gave off with an editorial against the draft. But as usual, they showed you only the front of the question. I am here to give you a good look at the behind.

They say drafting people into the army is undemocratic, un-American, and unproductive. My answer to that is, "Oh yeah?" But that is not my only reason. I believe that everybody should have the opportunity to serve this country and be ready to kill at the drop of a hat. I happen to be proud of my war injury. I have some shrapnel in my brain. Luckily, it landed in the part I do not use.

The draft is good for the country. It will not only help the unemployment situation, but it'll take crime off the streets and put it in the army where it belongs. Being drafted by the service is educational. It'll give you a great opportunity to learn all the words to the national anthem. If it wasn't for the draft, who'd fight the wars? I can't do it alone. Answer me that.

War promotes brotherhood. You learn to aim an M-1 rifle at those of a different race, creed, or color. Some people say the army is too strict. To that I say, "What do you put on a shingle?"

This station wants no draft. They want to deprive a boy of the army. The army is educational. The army teaches you how to do dental work—with the butt of a rifle. Also the army teaches you how to learn killing as a trade—which many people say is the coming thing. The army provides you with medical care, and even gives you free checkups to make sure you have not caught a romantic disease. You get to see army training films, all about bad ladies. These films are in glorious orange. And for protection, they put stuff in your food so that you will not get sexually excited and attack your duffel bag. The army makes a man out of you and prepares you for later life. They teach you how to crawl on your belly, which comes in handy when you're looking for a job in the private sector. The army is a good career. Our army has produced fine men such as General George C. Scott. I, Floyd R. Turbo, learned a lot in the army. It was a great experience, except for the bed wetter who slept on the top bunk.

The army taught me survival. I was in the Pacific. I learned how to survive in the jungle. I learned, for example, how to tell what time it is by making a sundial out of a dead person. I learned how to make beer out of bird droppings and also how to make a rubber girl out of an inner tube.

In conclusion, to sum it all up in a nutshell, I say we should not end the draft. We should increase it. We have a moral obligation to give Bob Hope soldiers to entertain. Fellow Americans, it is a honor to be drafted and to serve your country. Thank you, bye-bye, and buy bonds.

## Ed: Second Banana

*"I'll probably be rolling Johnny out in a wheelchair . . . The 'Tonight Show' is good for at least another five years, maybe longer. Who knows?"*        —Ed McMahon,
*St. Louis Globe Democrat,* 1973

Laurel and Hardy weren't teamed for this many years. Neither were Abbott and Costello. Don't even think about Martin and Lewis or Rowan and Martin. Have you considered that Ed McMahon and Johnny Carson will celebrate nearly thirty-five years together as host and sidekick when they retire from *The Tonight Show* in 1992?

Over the years we've seen him pitch insurance, beer, sweepstakes, and dog food. Professional huckster Ed McMahon admits he's good. "That's really what I am," he told *TV Guide.* "A good salesman. When I sold door to door, if they let me in, I sold eighty-five percent of the people." *(from the author's collection)*

Their professional relationship began in 1957 when McMahon, living in Philadelphia next door to Dick Clark, was called for an interview in New York about announcing a new show with Johnny Carson. "I met Johnny for about five minutes," McMahon says. "We were both looking out the window at the changing of a theater marquee sign across the street: *Bells Are Ringing* at the Schubert. We hardly even looked at each other." McMahon did not believe he had the job, but got called back to New York soon after, winning the prize: announcer for the ABC-TV show *Who Do You Trust?* with host Johnny Carson. The producers liked the "size difference" between the two, and felt they would work well together. When *The Tonight Show* came around, Carson insisted that McMahon remain as second banana, a title that McMahon has never found fault in.

"I'm also companion, assistant, consultant, and devil's advocate," he said in a 1971 interview. You might add straight man, resident huckster, and one of the most visible men on television these days. His role on *The Tonight Show* is "tough" he told Bob Costas on NBC-TV's *Later*: "It really is difficult. You have to be *in* when needed and *out* of the way when not. I can't get in [Johnny's] way but I have to help him. I've got to support him. Sort of the pusher who helps him get through the hour. But I can't look like I'm doing anything."

McMahon once referred to himself as a "thirty-year overnight success," because he's been in the business so long. From the time he was old enough to appreciate radio, he began to train himself as an announcer, he told writer Elise Cassel. "When I was

Johnny Carson surprised Ed McMahon with a visit to KNXT-TV's *Steve Edwards Show*, which celebrated McMahon's thirtieth anniversary in show business. *(courtesy of KNXT-TV, Los Angeles)*

twelve, I was already talking into a flashlight in front of mirrors and reading poetry aloud to my school class," he said.

He grew up in Lowell, Massachusetts, but was born in Detroit, Michigan, on March 6, 1923. He attended Boston College and began his broadcasting career at a Lowell radio station, WLLH. During World War II, McMahon became a pilot and flight instructor in the Marine Corps., and "emceed every show on the base," he said. "Wherever there was a microphone, I was."

He later attended the Catholic University of America and received his degree in speech and drama. Soon after, he took his first job at a television station in Philadelphia. The Korean War curtailed any plans he may have had, and he served as a fighter pilot until 1954.

Always a big fellow, the six-four Irish announcer has tried to keep his weight down, but he says his stature is the result of his Irish grandmother's cooking habits. He played football for Boston College in his late teens and tried to exercise as much as possible. Appearances have always been important to him, he has said. In 1973, he revealed that he traveled to the Bahamas "to get myself injected with those sheep cells," he told writer William Wolf. "You've heard about the treatment. It has really helped me to keep looking youthful. It's good for your skin, hair and in general revitalizes your body organs." Did you know Ed even wrote a diet book for those who were "born overweight," as he says, in the early seventies? His book *Slimming Down* provided advice about how to lose the unwanted pounds. His average weight over the years has been around 240 pounds. (His second book, *Here's Ed,* an autobiography as told to Carroll Carroll, was published in 1976.)

Now in the 1990s and at a turning point in his career, he will be leaving the *Tonight Show* but not necessarily any less busy. For years, McMahon has wanted to break into film acting. He had roles in motion pictures such as *The Incident, Slaughter's Big Rip-Off, Fun With Dick and Jane,* and *Butterfly,* and a TV movie, *The Star Maker.* His television roles include everything from a clown on early TV's *Big Top* to cameos on *CHiPs,* and *Alf.* He's hosted more than 150 episodes

Lucille Ball stars as Lucy Whittaker, with Vivian Vance as her best friend and Ed McMahon as her husband, Floyd, in the 1977 CBS-TV special *Lucy Calls the President. (from the author's collection)*

of *Star Search*, a successful syndicated talent show, and he continues to cohost specials with friend of many years Dick Clark.

McMahon's visibility has not waned in the three decades since he joined Johnny as the right-hand man. He's been a TV huckster in commercials and radio for Budweiser, Alpo dog food, and an array of insurance companies. Perhaps his most-recognized catchphrase outside of "Here's Johnny!" might be "You may have already won ten million dollars." He toured in a Las Vegas nightclub act for a while, and even appeared on Broadway briefly in *The Impossible Years*, substituting for Alan King. He contines to participate as second banana in Jerry Lewis's Muscular Dystrophy telethon each year, as well as making personal appearances in many holiday parades, such as Macy's Thanksgiving Day Parade and others.

Johnny makes an appearance on one of the early *Star Search* episodes hosted by Ed McMahon. *(from the author's collection)*

The personal life of Ed McMahon might be labeled as tumultuous as Johnny Carson's, in the marital department, that is. McMahon was separated in 1973 from his wife of twenty-seven years, the former Alyce Ferrell; they had four children. When he decided to move with *The Tonight Show* out to California, news reports indicated he was abandoning his wife, but he told the press his marriage was already in trouble. Amid a heavily publicized separation, McMahon was finally divorced in 1976. He remarried in 1976, to Victoria Valentine, and the couple adopted a little girl. They were divorced in 1989. These days, McMahon is single, dating, and tends to hit the front pages of the supermarket tabloids about as much as his partner, Johnny.

# A Few "Tea-Time Movies"

*Announcer: It's time once again, friends, for the Mighty Carson Art Players. One of the mainstays of daytime television is the late-afternoon movie. It's usually hosted by the happy-go-lucky bigmouth who's very happy to bring you the film feature, but a lot happier to bring you more commercials than you can find up Eighth Avenue. And now, your host . . . Art Fern.*

*"Hi there, Southland Viewers . . ."*

Hoot Gibson, Dean Stockwell, the Lane Sisters, and Cesar Romero in *Andy Hardy Gets a Girl in Trouble.*

Fuzzy Knight, Allen Jenkins, and Helen Twelvetrees in Otto Kruger's immortal classic *Ma & Pa Kettle Host an Orgy.*

Bob Steele, Spring Byington, Regis Toomey, and the Mormon Tabernacle Choir in *The Merry Widow Has a Change of Life.*

The Jackson Five, the Four Tops, the Three Stooges, the Doublemint Twins, and Furball the Wondercat in *Tarzan Breaks His Loincloth.*

Bobby Breen, June Frazee, Lash LaRue, and Beulah Bondi in *How Ya Gonna Keep 'Em Down on the Farm After They've Seen the Farm?*

Douglas Fairbanks, Jr., Junior Gilliam, Stu Gilliams, Stu Erwin, Irwin Corey, and Spurt the Wonderskunk in *Gidget Takes on Fort Ord.*

Jack Lemmon, Jack Haley, Hayley Mills, the Mills Brothers, Dr. Joyce Brothers, and Spawn the Wondercarp in *Dracula Gets Bombed on a Wino.*

Bess Flowers, Fifi D'Orsay, Guy Kibbee, and Cora Witherspoon in *Ma & Pa Kettle Join the Black Panthers.*

Spanky McFarland, Al McKrueger, Olga San Juan, Erich von Stroheim, and Fuzzy Knight in *I Was in Heat for an Artichoke.*

Benson Fong, Anna May Wong, Peter Chong, and Monatius Kummich in *Dr. Kildare Lances a Hickey.*

Ed Platt, Earl Flatt, Jack Sprat, Fats Domino, and Mervyn LeRoy in *How to Lose a Chinese Fortune (or Charley Chan Drops His Cookies).*

Eddie Foy, Myrna Loy, Clyde McCoy, Troy Donahue, and Mae Bush in *Joyce Brothers Finally Gets Hers.*

"Hello, Southland viewers . . ." Art Fern and the Matinee Lady introduce wacky films for the "Tea-Time Movie" sketch. *(courtesy of Steve Randisi)*

# "Doc"

In his hometown of Arlington, Oregon, his father, Carl Severinsen, was a dentist. Little Carl was nicknamed "Little Doc," and some time since he was young, part of the name eventually wore off.

Born on July 7, 1927, in the cattle country of Arlington, which contained a population of all of six hundred at that time, Little Doc Severinsen was small when his father would sit at the edge of his bed at night and play a violin. "He was a very good player, so it's a nice recollection to have," Doc Severinsen told Scott Yanow in an interview for *Down Beat* magazine. "I started on trumpet quite by accident. My father wanted me to be a violist like him, but I didn't take to it at all. In desperation he asked me what I would like to play and I picked the trombone because I liked the way it looked with the slide as played in the town band. There wasn't an extra one in town and I was too small for trombone anyway. But Herb Clarke, who worked at the Shell service station, had a cornet lying in his attic that I started with."

The seven-year-old developed his talents with the instrument rapidly, and after just three weeks, he was asked to join the local high school band. He insists, "If you had heard the band, you'd agree it was no big thing." But it was a start.

His father was a great source of creative energy for him, he says, in the development of his musical career. "He was a real taskmaster, a true perfectionist. I nearly went batty trying to please him, but he was my first inspiration."

He's more than Johnny Carson's stooge. Doc Severinsen is one of the country's leading trumpet players. *(from the the author's collection)*

Doc's biggest musical influences, like Harry James, Ziggy Elman, and Louis Armstrong, came by way of the radio when he was young. At the tender age of thirteen, he auditioned for Tommy Dorsey's band "as a fluke," he says of the experience, which left him with a growing ambition to play with Dorsey. By seventeen, he left home to tour with the Ted Fio Rito Orchestra, a short-lived gig. The army intervened during World War II, and after his discharge, Severinsen caught the tail end of the big-band era, joining Charlie Barnet a few times between 1947 and 1949.

While he was stationed at Fort Lewis, Washington, Doc heard his first Dizzy Gillespie records, which "spun my head around," he says in this 1970s interview using familiar beatnik vernacular. "[Dizzy] explored new territory. I tried to imitate Dizzy, to find out what this cat was layin' down. The guys in the band figured I was ready to join the Japanese army, the wild stuff I tried to play on my horn. I was really groovin' high."

He eventually sat in with Dorsey—a dream come true—Benny Goodman, Barnet, and others. "With Charlie Barnet, we never played one commercial tune," Doc says. "It was what you'd call a musician's band. Also it was my first mixed band, meaning I could sit next to some soul brothers and really swing."

In 1949, Severinsen landed in New York as a studio musician at NBC. He played in the house band when Steve Allen was hosting *Tonight!* and on through Jack Paar, and he caught the eye of music director Skitch Henderson.

"Skitch was always great to promote the fellows in the band," Severinsen told reporter Kim Plummer in 1981. "He kept raising my level of visibility to the point that it was understood that when he took off, I would take over." In 1967, he ended his term as the highly paid but anonymous studio musician and took over as the bandleader on *The Tonight Show*. Eventually, he became one of Johnny's stooges on the show, like a comic foil.

*Down Beat* reporter Scott Yanow asked for a few high points from his thousands of *Tonight Show* tapings. Severinsen brought to mind a few:

*I think the* Tonight Show *is the perfect home for any musician; it's certainly been a great place for me. I loved having Louis Armstrong, Dizzy Gillespie, Harry James and all the other musicians on. To have Joe Williams decide to fake something with the entire band faking a chart that you would swear they'd spent hours writing, was exciting. I'll never forget Miles Davis at the time his record* Bitches Brew *was out. Needless to say, his music was much too advanced for most people on the show. Miles came out, turned his back on the camera, and just wailed. I thought it was wonderful.*

After many years, Johnny finally asks Doc to Thanksgiving dinner in front of millions of viewers.

"What, do you think I'm gonna say 'Nooooo, Mr. Carson'?"

"So can you come?" Johnny asks.

"No."

Ahhhhhh, the seventies: peace, love, and extremely wide lapels. *(Personality Photos, Inc.)*

Leonard Slatkin, conductor for the St. Louis Symphony Orchestra, presents Doc Severinsen a cake on the anniversary of the trumpet player's fifth appearance with the symphony. *(from the author's collection)*

Severinsen will name a host of trumpeters he admires, like when the topic of his prime idol, Louis Armstrong, arises. "Satchmo Armstrong was the grandaddy of anybody who picks up the horn," he says. "I never felt I was of age until I heard Louis and could absorb his personality. The way he would feel the music . . . when Louis played his horn or when he sang, he said it all." He says he likes Freddie Hubbard, Wynton Marsalis, and a fellow by the name of Chris Botti he caught doing a club date in Indianapolis a few years back, "just knocked my socks off!"

With threads as loud as his trumpet, the Liberace syndrome of dressing-to-be-noticed has become part of his personality, on the show and off. *Everyone* asks about his wardrobe. *Everyone* comments about it. And he tires of it sometimes.

As the story goes, one year on *The Tonight Show* he began wearing one wild necktie after another. Johnny began to make "No-Pest Strip" jokes about them, and soon he graduated to loud shirts, and so on. "My clothes have become sort of a trademark, and I guess I'm sort of stuck with it," he says. "But I really like dressing that way. Gives me a lift. I have most of 'em custom made, but I usually pick up some flashy additions when I shop around on the road."

After nearly nineteen years as music director to the NBC band, Severinsen finally recorded the ensemble in 1986, which resulted in two Grammy awards. Doc also splits his time between the show and his fusion group, Xebron, which tours the country. The name comes from "a little place I created in my mind to get away from the world," he says.

His style varies incredibly. Although perhaps best known for his superb trumpet playing, he's one of today's premier instrumentalists with more than thirty recordings ranging from big-band sounds to Dixieland, traditional jazz, and country music. He accompanies a battery of symphony orchestras each year as a guest conductor/performer, including the Boston Pops, the Chicago Symphony, the St. Louis Symphony Orchestra, and the New York Philharmonic, to name just a few. He has been voted "Top Brass Player" no fewer than ten times in *Playboy*'s music poll.

Along with the bright wardrobe, the other bright spots in his life are his five children from previous marriages. His second marriage ended in divorce in 1976 in a messy battle that was spread throughout the press. In 1980, he married his third wife, television writer Emily Marshall, who was working as the secretary to *Tonight Show* executive producer Fred de Cordova at the time they met.

Doc Severinsen plays at the 1985 Veiled Prophet Fair in St. Louis, one of the country's largest July Fourth celebrations. *(photo by Tim Vizer)*

# Doc Severinsen Selected Discography

Facets—Amherst 3319

The Tonight Show Band—Amherst 3311

The Tonight Show Band, Vol. II—Amherst 3312

Night Journey—Epic 34078

Once More . . . With Feeling—Amherst 94405

Merry Christmas From—Amherst 94406

Trumpet Spectacular—Telarc 30223 with Charlie Barnet

Bebop Spoken Here—Capitol 11061 with Mike Bryan

Mike Bryan Sextet—Storyville 4015 with Stan Getz

Big Band Bossa Nova—Verve 8494 with various artists

Big Band Hit Parade—Telarc CD-80177

# Carnac the Magnificent

ANNOUNCER: *I have in my hand an envelope; a child of four can plainly see these envelopes are hermetically sealed. They've been kept since noon today in a mayonnaise jar on Funk & Wagnalls' porch. No one—but no one!—knows the contents. In his mystical, magical, and borderline divine way, Carnac will now ascertain the answers, having never heard the questions. . . .*

Sort of like psychic *Jeopardy,* in his greatness the bumbling telepath-in-a-turban could "divine answers" from a white envelope held at his forehead, without seeing the questions. Methodically, the envelope was torn at the end, Carnac would blow into the envelope and pull out the question to which he foretold an answer. And if the crowd booed the Great One in his mighty wisdom, he might have cursed in response: "May a kangaroo punch out your erogenous zone," or "May a love-starved fruitfly molest your sister's nectarines," and possibly, "May your youngest son run the spit-shine concession at a leather bar." One night it was, "May a nearsighted sand flea suck syrup off your short stack."

## Answers (Questions on opposite page)

*"Silence Please . . ."*

1. Moonies
2. A cat and your wife
3. Lollipop
4. Preparation H and take-home pay
5. Dairy Queen
6. The American people
7. Sis Boom Bah
8. A B C D E F G
9. Mr. Coffee
10. The Loch Ness Monster
11. Mount Baldy
12. The zip code
13. A linen closet
14. 20/20
15. "Thank you, PaineWebber" (sic)
16. Coal Miner's Daughter
17. Real People
18. NAACP FBI IRS
19. I give a damn
20. Hasbro
21. Spam and Jim Bakker
22. Ovaltine
23. Bungy diving and a date with Geraldo
24. Hop Sing
25. All systems go
26. 10–4
27. persnickety
28. "These are a few of my favorite things"
29. Hell or high water

Announcer: *"I hold in my hand . . . the last envelope."*

30. A pair of Jordache jeans and a bread box

The most popular Carnac of all:
ANSWER: Sis Boom Bah.
QUESTION: Describe the sound of a sheep blowing up.

## Carnac's Questions

1. Name a religion that drops its pants.
2. Name something you put out at night and someone who won't.
3. What happens when someone stomps on your lolly?
4. What can you depend on for shrinking?
5. What do you call a gay milkman?
6. Name the loser in the 1976 presidential race.
7. Describe the sound you hear when a sheep blows up.
8. What were some of the earlier forms of Preparation H?
9. Name the father of Mrs. Olsen's illegitimate baby.
10. Who will they find sooner than Jimmy Hoffa?
11. How do you play piggyback with Telly Savalas?
12. What do CIA agents have to remember to go to the bathroom?
13. What do gay Irish guys come out of?
14. What will a gallon of gas cost by next year?
15. What might a girl say at a stockbrokers' orgy?
16. Where can you pick up a nasty soot-rash?
17. What do lonely inflatable people buy for companionship?
18. How do you spell naacpfoiirs?
19. What did it say in the Beaver's will?
20. How does Tito Jackson get work?
21. Name two things that'll be in the can for the next eighteen years.
22. Describe Oprah Winfrey in high school.
23. Name two things that end with a jerk on your leg.
24. Name a prison for one-legged people.
25. What happens if you take a Sinutab, a Maalox, and a Feen-a-mint?
26. How do a big guy and a little guy split fourteen bucks?
27. How do you get paid when you're picking snicketies?
28. What do you say to a doctor who's wearing a rubber glove?
29. Name two things you really don't want in your underwear.
30. Name two places where you stuff your buns.

# Tommy Newsom

❝ *Things never go right with Tommy . . . his inflatable woman has PMS.* ❞

—Johnny Carson

In a *Tonight Show* parody segment of the television show *This is Your Life*, Johnny, acting as moderator Ralph Edwards, stopped the show, sat Tommy Newsom down and began a tribute that put it all in perspective. The opening went a bit like this:

> *Born Thomas "Tapioca" Newsom in a sleepy southern seaport town of Portsmouth, Virginia, on February 25, 1929, appropriately enough, the year of the Great Depression.*
>
> *You were born to a proud, but dull, Virginia family. Tommy, you are a direct descendant of a boring Revolutionary war hero, Nathan Hale Newsom, who when captured by the British, said, "I regret that I have no life to give for my country."*
>
> *And at the end of age two, you were abandoned by your parents at Pismo Beach, California, and raised by a herd of wild clams. The year was 1941. War broke out, and you answered your nation's call. You volunteered for an elite commando unit, the Polyester Berets . . .*

The character that is Tommy Newsom is one that's been cultivated over the years and molded into this glob of, well, nothingness. *This Is Your Life* correctly reported his age and birthplace, but disregard the clams, he says.

According to Johnny Carson, Tommy is a dull, square, bland individual who plays many instruments on the show, sits visibly behind in the bandstand, and fills in for Doc when the bandleader's absent. If you think of it, *nothing* could be dull about someone who's worked with *The Tonight Show* for so many years. Ohhh, the stories he must have. Cautious in nature, he doesn't wish to expound much about the band's unofficial watering hole currently known as "Chadney's," across the street from NBC. "The band has been known to raise a glass on the break occasionally," he says. Many ticket-holders waiting outside NBC have witnessed a sweating band member or two, hustling across the busy street in his dark blue blazer, out of breath and making a mad dash to the studio. "We have to get to the studio fifteen minutes before airtime," he says.

Lack of personality and his television persona aside, the *real* Tommy Newsom—yes, that's his real name—is a kind, gentle, mostly serious man with a Virginia coastal accent and a face that resembles everybody's favorite uncle's. His sense of humor is actually sharp, and when he fills in on Doc Severinsen's days off, his natural wit shines every time Johnny asks him a simple question like "What's up, Tommy?" or "So where's Doc tonight?" When quizzed if Doc stays in touch during his vacations, Newsom said, "I don't even think he watches the show." Johnny doesn't banter long, for fear that Tommy may get an abundance of laughs, outdoing the monologue. But TV's master of monotony packs a quick wallop with whatever ad-libs he delivers. And they *are* ad-libs, he insists. "I don't even look at [Johnny's] cue cards, 'cause I don't want to know," he says. "It's best off the top of my head. Johnny likes that, and he seems to respond to it. Sometimes I say something off the wall, and it tickles him."

He may not be the simpleton Johnny describes, but he does admit at least some of legend is valid. "I don't take Johnny's comments personally," he says of the streamlined insults aimed at his supposed neutral nature. "It's like they're talkin' about a third person," Newsom says. "Of course, there is a kernel of truth in all of those things. I don't lead a very exciting existence. Not anything the press would love. If they relied on me for news, they would die.

"I hope I'm a *little* more animated than they portray me," he says. "It's good ammunition for the writers. It doesn't bother me, but it used to bother some of my mother's friends, I remember. You try an' tell 'em it's just a show, but that's not sufficient."

Johnny chats with band member Tommy Newsom, whom he's called "the ghost of clothes past." *(Personality Photos, Inc.)*

Artistically, Newsom plays the clarinet, the flute, and the piano—"badly," he says. He attended the college of William and Mary but was graduated from the Peabody Conservatory of Music in Baltimore, where he studied piano and also saxophone. Following three years as a member of the Air Force Band from 1953 to 1956, he received an M.A. in music education from Columbia University. He and his wife of many years, Pat, have two grown children, Mark and Candy. The Newsoms live quietly, of course, in Tarzana, California.

Over the years, Newsom has lent his musical talents to the bands of Benny Goodman, Les Elgart, and Skitch Henderson. He has composed and arranged for Goodman, Henderson, Woody Herman, Charlie Byrd, and André Kostelanetz. During the summer of 1962, just prior to Johnny Carson's arrival as the new host of *The Tonight Show*, Newsom joined the group, when Doc was a member of the band as well. In 1968 he was appointed assistant musical director, which was quite a departure for Newsom since he had always been "a spear carrier, or a follower or member of the band—never a leader, until this job," he points out. Over the last thirty years, audiences have recognized him almost as much as Severinsen, and sometimes with more enthusiasm and affection than his bandleader boss.

"The majority of people identify with me," he says. "You know, the person who is the brunt of someone's humor. It's more typical than say, a flamboyant person."

When he's not rehearsing with the band at NBC or noodlin' around with instruments at home, Tommy sits in with a quintet at a nearby Simi Valley cowboy bar and fills his weekends with work. When Carson retires, so will Newsom—only from the show, he's quick to say. "I'm not retiring by my own volition," says Newsom with a tinge of protest. "They may get a new band, but I'll go on to do other things."

# Public-Service Announcements

**"The following is a Public-Service Announcement . . ."**

*This is Johnny Carson here. If you've been following the news, you'll know that Humphrey the Humpback Whale went the wrong way and was trapped in the San Fernando River for three long weeks. Because of this, the unlucky mammal will be too late for the mating season off the coast of Mexico.*

*This is an urgent plea. If you manage an aquatic theme park such as Sea World or Marineland, or if you just own a female whale in heat, you can help Humphrey. Contact:*

Tail for the Whale
Baja, CA

**"The following is a Public-Service Announcement . . ."**

*Hi. This is Johnny Carson reminding you that the days when it was a good idea to donate your body to medical science are long past. Nowadays, every medical school in the country is filled to the rafters with more cadavers than it can possibly use.*

*But you can still donate your body to a worthy cause . . . to your local fast-food restaurant, where it will be used as a speed bump in their parking lot. In this way, you'll be remembered by your loved ones every time they come in for some burgers, drive through too fast over you, and wreck their front-wheel alignment. For a donor card you can keep with you at all times in your wallet, send to:*

Jack-in-the-Asphalt
Studio City, CA 91604

**"The following is a Public-Service Announcement . . ."**

*Hi, this is Johnny Carson making a plea directly to you women in Beverly Hills. Do you realize that there are women in rural communities of your country less fortunate than you? Ladies who live hundreds of miles from a plastic surgeon? Yes, I'm talking about flat-chested farm wives. Won't you help out? Send your extra silicone to:*

Boobs for Rubes
Twiggy, KS 80725

# Acknowledgments

## "My thanks to . . ."

All of those individuals listed here, and those I may have inadvertently missed, I can only present you with a warm smile and words of gratitude. Each time I pick up this book, I will recall your kind assistance . . . and in some instances, the arm-twisting I had to employ.

Foremost, I would like to thank Johnny Carson for giving me the chance; I'm sure he can recall an individual or two who gave *him* a break early in his career. And my advice to him: Please, Johnny, write a book. I'll be the first to buy it.

Secondly, I am grateful to many individuals: my research consultant, Steve Randisi; my "girl Friday," Sandy Mailliard; my longtime favorite librarian, Carol Brady, who nurtured my interest in books when I was a youngster who could hardly see over the counter—her smile always brought me back; and to my editor, John Michel, a Johnny Carson fan who exercised hair-pulling patience throughout this project. And for those whom I interviewed, all mentioned within the text—and those who wished their names withheld—I couldn't have written the book without you. (Moreover, please accept my heartfelt appreciation for your decision to provide a few words rather than forego the opportunity, fearing repercussions within your friendships simply because this was "a book about Johnny Carson." Maybe your faith in positive, fair books will be restored.)

Additionally, but not of lesser importance by any means, I would like to offer applause to: Ken Beck; Noel Blanc; Tom Brown; Bruce Button; Mickey Carroll; my parents Gerald and Blanche Cox; Jean Cox; Ramona Christophel; Jeff Forrester; Paul and Ruth Henning; Dayna Hooper; Kevin Marhanka; Gary Meyer; Scott Michaels; Jim Mullholland; Tim Neeley; Michael Pietsch; John Pertzborn (KSDK-TV); Herbie J. Pilato; Pam Reichman; Helen Sanders; Billie Freebairn-Smith; Shannon Showalter; Dave Strauss; Julie Sullivan (NBC legal department); Carey Thorpe; Joe Wallison; Dan Weaver; Elaine Willingham; Dave Woodman.

Special thanks goes to those extraordinary writers who contributed their talents via wonderfully insightful guest chapters for this book: John Lofflin, Joe Rhodes, and Neil Shister. To you colleagues, I tip my hat.

Without the astonishing variety of illustrations provided by Howard Frank and his father, this book would not be complete. His media archive is a nonpareil. (Personality Photos, Inc., P.O. Box 50, Brooklyn, NY 11230. Inquiries send S.A.S.E.) Also, many thanks to Wide World Photo, Globe Photos, Doc Severinsen, the National Broadcasting Company, Inc., the NBC graphic-arts department.

Grateful acknowledgment is made to the following to reprint special materials: *TV Guide* and News America Publications, Inc., Radnor, PA.; NBC Legal; Bob Costas and Betelgeuse Productions, Inc.

Lastly, and most importantly, grateful acknowledgement is made to Johnny Carson for permission to reprint his routines;

*"G'night, Folks!"*

# About the Author

Stephen Cox was born five years after Johnny Carson assumed *The Tonight Show*. He admits staying up much too late on school nights to watch Johnny, and doesn't regret an hour of it. An avid television and movie buff, Cox feels fortunate that he's had the opportunity to turn his hobby into a career of writing about media and the personalities he's enjoyed most. He graduated from Park College in Kansas City, Missouri, with a B.A. in journalism and communication arts. Currently, Burbank, California, is his home.

Other books by Cox include: *The Beverly Hillbillies, The Munchkins Remember The Wizard of Oz and Beyond, The Munsters, The Addams Chronicles*, and with John Lofflin *The Official Abbott & Costello Scrapbook*.